A Mother
and Daughter
Guidebook

ASPERGER'S
IN
PINK

for Raising
(or being!)
a Girl with
Asperger's

Julie
Clark

FUTURE HORIZONS INC.

Arlington, Texas

ASPERGER'S IN PINK

All marketing and publishing rights guaranteed to and reserved by:

FUTURE HORIZONS INC.

721 W. Abram Street
Arlington, Texas 76013
800-489-0727
817-277-0727
817-277-2270 (fax)
E-MAIL: *info@FHautism.com*
www.FHautism.com

Book design © TLC Graphics, *www.TLCGraphics.com*
Cover by: Monica Thomas; Interior by: Erin Stark

Printed in Canada

Publisher's Cataloging-In-Publication Data

Clark, Julie.

Asperger's in pink : a mother and daughter guidebook for raising (or being!) a girl with Asperger's / Julie Clark.

p. ; cm.

Includes bibliographical references and index.

ISBN: 978-1-935274-10-0

1. Asperger's syndrome in children—Popular works. 2. Developmentally disabled children—Popular works. 3. Parenting—Popular works. 4. Parents of autistic children—Popular works. 5. Mothers and daughters—Popular works. I. Title.

RJ506.A9 C53 2010

618.92/858/8

For my amazing, beautiful daughter,
and her father, my husband and teammate

Acknowledgments

Recently, I thanked a friend for her support along the way, and she quickly dismissed it, thinking it didn't amount to much. But kind words do add up, and every person who has uttered even a few words of encouragement along this journey is forever imprinted on my heart. Thank you.

First and foremost, unending thanks goes out to Wayne Gilpin, along with everyone at Future Horizons, for taking on our story, and being so wonderful to work with! I can't say enough, and am forever grateful. A special note of thanks goes to my editor, Kelly Gilpin. "Thanks for everything" just doesn't seem to cut it.

Thanks to Ellen Notbohm, for a timely boost of courage with a side of wisdom every "young" author needs. Thanks to Rudy Simone, for her uplifting words to me, and for writing the foreword. Much appreciation goes to Dr. Cara Regan, who has provided wisdom and support. A condensed "thanks" goes to Kim Casey, whose gentle pushes of encouragement throughout the decades continue to provide me with confidence to be true to who I am. And to Sally, whose friendship I will always, always treasure.

I'd also like to take a moment to express appreciation for experts in the field, such as Dr. Tony Attwood, whose work continues to help families like ours. Likewise, helpful online sources, such as the Bridge newsletter (a publication of the Advocacy Center).

Endless gratitude goes to my husband, who is a large force behind *Asperger's in Pink*. I could not have written this without his support. And to my daughter, the best daughter anyone could ask for, who has permitted me to share a glimpse into her world with the world. I don't know what I would do without her.

Kristina would like to thank all of her friends who support her for who she is and what is within her, without judging her, and she would especially like to thank her first ever "real" best friend. Thank you.

Table of Contents

Section I—The Diagnostic Process

Section II—School

Asperger's in Pink

Foreword

"She doesn't seem autistic to me," is a statement that Julie Clark hears again and again when she tells people her daughter has Asperger's Syndrome. "I didn't know girls could have it" or "she sounds just like my kid," are other common responses. This skepticism even occurs after a positive, professional diagnosis. Ironically, one of the biggest challenges in being high-functioning lies in convincing others we have challenges. Most people don't realize that autism is a not only a long spectrum but also a wide one, and different people sit on different parts of that landscape. "She's not autistic; she's spoiled," Julie also hears, a mild cousin of the "refrigerator mother" theory of autism. Even the best parents can be accused of being part of the problem rather than the solution. Even the most well-meaning individuals may dispute a diagnosis of AS, in an effort to simplify or normalize the situation.

There is a mindset that naming something will give it more power. Naming *is* a powerful thing—"Asperger's Syndrome" aligns us with a group, it gives us a backdrop and a catalog of information. So many AS females don't have the name; Asperger's manifests differently in girls, often resulting in multiple misdiagnoses and not having access to the proper care and support. Diagnosis is the beginning of a labyrinthine, bureaucratic but sometimes very effective system of support for a child. Without diagnosis, girls are left with the wondering and the questions. They don't have the subculture to turn to for answers and support. In short, they struggle.

Kristina, the real life star of *Asperger's in Pink,* is a little girl who has to contend with many struggles but is too young to know it yet. She doesn't understand that other children don't have the same perspectives, the same talents and the same sensitivities. Or if she does see it, she thinks it is because she is gifted and they are not. In many ways she is right, but to be intellectually gifted is often to be emotionally, socially, and sensorially challenged. Often the drawbacks for an AS girl only become painfully obvious when she hits adolescence or puberty. When her childhood friends, if she had any, may begin to distance themselves from her quirks and align themselves with other, less awkward, more popular girls. This is when the person with Asperger's begins to realize the downside of "different," when to be different almost guarantees isolation and bullying.

Those involved in the life of a young child need full understanding of Asperger's so the child isn't blamed for their behavior, resulting in guilt and confusion. These can lead to lifelong depression and anxiety, which may, in the case of older girls looking for diagnosis, throw counselors and psychologists completely off the trail of AS, causing them to treat the symptoms rather than identify the source. Kristina's mother Julie knows this and does her best to stay one step ahead of the game. Battling apathy, ignorance, and indifference, she tries to pull everyone else in her daughter's world up to speed. Like the mothers of some of our more well-known Aspergirls, such as Temple Grandin and Liane Holliday Willey, Julie is a mother who knows, and always knew, that her child is "super special," that she is worth taking the time for. She fights daily so her daughter doesn't have to, so that the weight of being different doesn't cause her daughter to lose the spring in her step. Not all girls with Asperger's are so lucky. Many have had parents who did not have the ability, the wherewithal, the education, or the patience to understand their child. Some had children on the spectrum before the diagnosis existed. Julie Clark took the time to investigate Asperger's Syndrome with the tenacity of a detective on the trail. She followed the clues, she enlisted the aid of professionals, and then she diligently monitored the progress of her daughter's education and care. She wanted to trust other people to have her daughter's best interest at heart, but unfortunately some people who are entrusted to sculpt an inclusive, enlightened world for our kids sometimes find it easier to leave the odd ones out of the reindeer games. Julie also eloquently illustrates how just one caring, thoughtful, engaged soul can make a vast world of difference in a child's life and the lives of her family.

Kristina is very lucky to have *both* parents take the time to actively be involved in all facets of her life and well-being. Usually one parent or caregiver has the burden of not only educating themselves about Asperger's, but everyone else around them as well, including their partner. Julie and her husband Andrew were likewise fortunate that Kristina's pediatrician took their AS suspicions seriously, and became a crucial ally early on. The doctor was easy to convince. Other, less knowledgeable people proved to be more difficult but just as crucial to bring on board. Julie's description of an interrogative phone call from a case worker was chilling to me because we've all been put on the defensive by those that don't do their homework. Ms. Clark stresses the importance of communication and cohesion between everyone involved, so no one is working at cross-purposes, so they are supporting rather than defeating each other's efforts. She warns that you may have to be a squeaky wheel to get that communication, and to keep the whole machine from grinding to a halt. She gives advice no one gave her, and although she laments the lack of a handbook of terminology, she provides us with the beginnings of one in this book.

As Ms. Clark so eloquently points out, many of Kristina's good points were not only overlooked, but were almost treated as problems or evidence of a disturbed nature. Most people think it isn't "normal" for a three-year-old to be a self-taught reader. But in the world of *female* Asperger's, my research shows that it is quite common. Barring learning disabilities, so is burning through assignments at a rate so rapid teachers can't give them out fast enough, and correcting adults when they are wrong. These should be signs that there is a gifted, unusual child on the scene. The lack of social graces and eye contact, taking things literally, adverse reactions to sensory overload, those of us familiar with AS know these are garden variety traits, but for the uninformed world, they are evidence of a slow, spoiled, or unsocialized child. This is the universal Aspergian experience of being misunderstood. Julie reminds us that although the child's blunt honesty is often interpreted as disrespect, it should be applauded, for although it does make for some difficult interactions, this is an attribute of a leader, not a follower.

Julie's humility and the admission that her experiences are subjective are part of what makes their story so universal—we all feel very alone at times in this journey. She reminds us that kids with AS aren't the only ones who struggle for a social life; parents and caregivers can also become isolated. Julie wants no thanks, no sympathy, she is plaintively calling out to people—family, teachers, psychologists, friends—to just take a moment and hear this story, in order to make it easier for the next family, the next Kristina. I was riveted from the moment I started this book until I put it down at the last page. Story after story, milestone after milestone, I was with Julie and her family. I felt their fear, their worries, but mostly I felt incredibly relieved and gratified that Kristina has such a champion on her side. I wish all little girls with Asperger's did.

This book is going to be both lighthouse and life raft for parents, giving them something to aim for and the way to get there. Parents of an AS child (whether girl or boy) who are trying to procure a diagnosis or who have a diagnosis but don't know what to do next, Ms. Clark has provided you with a map. Kristina will have another series of chapters to go through and I almost heard the word "sequel" in my mind when I finished this book.

Asperger's in Pink

One thing to remember is that while female AS is different than male, no two girls will be exactly alike either. Some will want friends, others won't. Some make eye contact, others can't. Some will be verbal, others visual, and so on. And as Kristina gets older, and becomes a teenager, she too will change. I'm looking forward to catching up with her in the future. I'm sure it will be a challenging but happy one. Thanks to books like this and the parents and professionals who take the time to read them, many more little Aspergirls will have the future they deserve.

— RUDY SIMONE
*Author of Aspergirls: Empowering Females with
Asperger's Syndrome and Asperger's on the Job: Must-Have
Advice for People with Asperger's or High-Functioning Autism,
and their Employers, Educators, and Advocates*

Before You Begin

"I feel like any other ordinary kid,
and I want to be respected like one."

— Kristina

ASPERGER'S, IN A NUTSHELL

Asperger's Syndrome Disorder is an Autism Spectrum Disorder. Autism, itself, varies greatly, with some individuals always needing attentive care, while yet others with milder forms, such as those with Asperger's, live "normal" lives, completing college, marrying, and going on to raise families.

Once thought to affect one out of 166 people, the CDC now estimates that autism affects one out of every 110 individuals. It is not yet understood whether instances of autism are on the rise, or if it is simply an increasing understanding of autism that is resulting in better, and more widespread, diagnoses.

Although more males than females are diagnosed with Asperger's, the exact ratio is unclear. However, both males and females share certain traits. Markers and traits of Asperger's generally include lack of eye contact, inadequate social ability, strict adherence to routine, sensory integration difficulties, lack of empathy, intense interest in a limited number of subjects, rigidity, and a literal way of thinking.

Although Asperger's Syndrome was brought to light by a Viennese physician, Hans Asperger, in 1944, it would not be until 1994, a full fifty years later, that this syndrome would be recognized in the United States, and added to the DSM-IV.

As of this writing, the exact cause for Asperger's Syndrome is unknown. It is suspected genetics play a role, as at least one parent or close family member typically exhibits a marker or two of the syndrome. Regardless, the cause is considered neurological, not psychological in nature.

As with classic autism, there is no known cure. In fact, many individuals believe a cure is unnecessary. Many desire to look at Asperger's simply as another way of thinking.

PINK PEARLS

"Pink Pearls" pulls out the key points and ideas presented throughout each chapter. Located at the end of each chapter, Pink Pearls is divided into three sections. The first section speaks to the parents, referring to them as "caregivers," as some children are not under the direct supervision of their parents. The second section is addressed to those outside the immediate family, such as educators and extended family members. The target audience for this section reflects the content of the particular chapter. The third section is a one-sentence wish or a sentence of thankfulness, mentioning an available tool/service deemed extremely helpful or desirable. (A fourth section, "For Everyone," is interjected when applicable.)

TO PROTECT AND RESPECT

In order to protect and respect the privacy of the individuals and establishments mentioned, names, places, and identifying characteristics have been changed.

Preface

THE LIFE CYCLE OF A DOUGHNUT

Kristina's eyes widened as her father suggested a trip to the new doughnut shop across town. It was a perfect proposal for a daddy-daughter date. For me, it was a perfect plan for some bonding time, as well as some quiet time for myself.

After zipping up her pink parka, Kristina griped as we fiddled with her mittens. Not quite five, she still struggled with arranging them "just so" on her small fingers. In Kristina's world, there would never be a need for mittens or gloves.

"Do you want us to bring you back anything?" asked Andrew.

"No, I don't think so. Thanks, though," I responded.

Andrew and Kristina made their way to car. Being the gentleman he is, he opened the door for our princess, allowing her to plop easily inside her carriage.

A short while later, the glowing neon lights reflected in Kristina's eyes. The radiant sign indicated fresh, warm doughnuts inside. The warm, sweet smell of the confections filled the small building. So many choices. So many options. Kristina rushed up to the glass encasing the workroom. A small, raised walkway allowed smaller customers to watch the baking process. Trays upon trays of raw dough circled around, until making their way onto a metal conveyor belt, making each step of the process, from dough to dining, easy to follow.

Kristina stood mesmerized, as Andrew explained it all to her. As she listened, Kristina chose to lock her eyes on one particular doughnut, following it to the end. A glass case full of sweet choices greeted them at the conclusion of the "tour." True to form, Kristina settled on a simple doughnut with sprinkles, while her father chose something slightly more complex.

The two sat down, enjoying time together. Such a simple night out, firming the bond between father and daughter. After putting jackets and caps back on, Kristina took one more glance through the large windows, once again following a doughnut to the end.

All too soon, bedtime came calling, time to head back to the carriage, back home.

"Did you have a good time, tonight?" asked Andrew.

"Oh, yes, Daddy. When can we go back?"

"Oh, I don't know. Next time, how 'bout we bring your mother?"

"I think Mommy would like that. I can't wait to tell her all about the life cycle of a doughnut!"

Andrew sat there, eyes fixed on the road, his mind ruminating over her choice of words. *The life cycle of a doughnut.* He'd never thought of it like that before.

"That's a clever way to put it," Andrew mentioned.

"Well, you see it starting out, then it turns into a doughnut, then you eat it. It's a life cycle," quipped Kristina.

"You know, you're right."

Not yet in school, Kristina made the connection. Somehow, somewhere, Kristina picked up on the concept of a life cycle. Kristina being Kristina, it was nothing but common sense.

As often said, common sense is the least common sense of them all.

Introduction

"Your child has Asperger's? I know someone at work who has a kid with Asperger's. When was your son diagnosed?"

"We don't have a son. Our daughter has Asperger's."

"Your daughter? Huh. I thought mostly boys had Asperger's."

I bite my tongue, as I feel sarcasm rising in me, wanting to say, "Most, not all. That makes the remainder of 'most' girls." But I don't share my thoughts. I simply reply, "Yes, I know. My husband and I have yet to know anyone else who has a girl with Asperger's."

I finish exchanging pleasantries with the well-meaning individual, and go on my way. At home, I plop on my couch, sinking into its oversized pillows, sulking at the general lack of understanding surrounding my family.

Sure, Asperger's is diagnosed less frequently in girls than boys. However, according to Dr. Tony Attwood, a respected expert on Asperger's Syndrome, the ratio is thought to be 4:1, similar to classic autism. But that doesn't mean girls with Asperger's are any less affected than boys. Still, according to research, the ratio of boys to girls referred for assessment is much higher, 10:1, with the gap narrowing as girls approach adulthood.

Simply put, girls often go undiagnosed much longer than their male counterparts.

It is no wonder we feel we have to defend Kristina's diagnosis.

Over and over again.

"Oh, come on," another says, "all kids are picky. All kids are shy. All kids speak their minds. All kids have favorite things. All kids…"

All kids do not have Asperger's.

Meanwhile, as I reflect on the words of those who question my daughter's diagnosis, I want to crawl into a hole. Or pack up my family, and head to the hills. Many, many times, it seems as if we are in it alone. Sometimes, it even seems as if it's all a ruse, and Kristina is like any other perfectly "normal" child. Sometimes I wonder if her idiosyncrasies *are* our doing. But then something will happen, something in life that will make Asperger's appear alive, well, and inescapable, like thick snowflakes in January.

In writing this book, my hope is to shed a little light on what life is like raising a young girl with Asperger's Syndrome Disorder. This is our story, told from a mother's heart. Our experience isn't any less, or even any greater, than anyone else's in our situation.

Kristina was diagnosed with Asperger's Syndrome Disorder during first grade. To date, five professionals concur with her diagnosis. I am including that bit to assure you that her diagnosis is firm, our experiences real.

In talking with Kristina about this book, she, like any other kid, has bounced around from excited to anxious. Excited she's having a book written about *her*. Anxious her parents will do something to embarrass her. After all, she is on the brink of middle school, where parents embarrassing their children becomes nothing short of an art form. Still, it is very important to Kristina that Asperger's be understood—and especially how it relates to girls.

Kristina, like any other ten year old, loves to read, play, and watch TV. Like any other ten year old, she doesn't like chores—or brussel sprouts. In other words, in many ways, Kristina is just like any other daughter. Her desire is for others to understand that kids like her are much like any other kids. However, Kristina understands there are things about her that do make her different. It is important to Kristina that folks understand these differences, and, as a result, accept her for who she is. After all, it doesn't matter to her if her friends have special needs or not. We've taught her to look at the heart, not externals.

She expects the same.

If you would ask her about Asperger's, she would put her hands on her hips, cross her eyebrows, and firmly tell you it is not a disease, and she is not sick. She would also tell you there is nothing wrong with having Asperger's. She might even ask you "what's the big deal" about Asperger's anyway. She would tell you that kids with Asperger's are like any other kids. She would tell you there is nothing wrong with her, though she is a bit different.

Let's not lose sight that these folks with Asperger's are just that—folks. People. Relatives. Individuals with souls just like anyone else. I hope this book provides you with a peek at the heart of a young girl with Asperger's Syndrome, and her family.

Here is a glimpse of Asperger's in pink.

SECTION
ONE

The
Diagnostic
Process

Chapter One

The Road to Diagnosis

Why do kids always ask, "Are we there yet?" when they can look out the window and see for themselves?

— KRISTINA

Last night, I sat across the table from my ten-year-old daughter. Dinner was ending, and it was about time to leave for her school's art show. This was Kristina's last, as middle school starts up this fall. As our dinner conversation wrapped up, she tilted her blonde head, looked away from me, and lifted a hand in disgust.

Here it comes.

"Mommy, I just can't look at you anymore!" Kristina declared.

I sat there clueless as to this latest proclamation. It was not unusual for similar comments to proceed an unacceptable dinner. And I'm not talking just about the food. It could be how the napkin is lying on the table, or the order of the silverware.

Or using the "wrong" silverware.

However, tonight was her favorite, so that couldn't be it. Conversation ran smoothly, so it wasn't something I said. I already asked her about my new haircut, and she was uninterested. So, I just sat back, waiting for it to come.

Kristina is not one to hold anything in.

"It's your *hair*!" she began. "It's … got … gray … all … over-it-now. Ugh! Mommy, I just can't look at it anymore. It's just not right!"

Andrew sat there silent, as did I. In our household, it's a well-known fact that new haircuts magically sprout more gray. In our household, it's also a well-known fact that I'm hanging onto the illusion of remaining a natural brunette.

Andrew and I exchanged a smile, chalking another "encouraging" comment up to Kristina being Kristina.

A few years back, sitting in the same chair, across from the same child, Kristina offered up more wisdom. I was in the middle of a diet, and felt pretty proud of my progress, having only a few more pounds to go. As I mumbled something to Andrew about wanting to whittle a little more from my waistline, he encouraged me, telling me I looked just fine.

Kristina, on the other hand, didn't see things the same way. She sat for a moment, intense in thought. Finally, a large grin graced her thin lips, and, with a matter-of-fact tone, she verbalized her assessment of the situation.

"You know, Mommy, when you sit that way, you *do* look fat!"

At least we weren't at Grandma's house.

At least she did not say that to Grandma.

This morning, as we waited for the school bus, I asked Kristina about last night's conversation. She said the gray in my hair "freaks her out." I am not supposed to turn gray. It goes against her perception of me. In her mind, it also means I'm getting older.

Life with a child who has Asperger's Syndrome Disorder can be … interesting. Having a daughter with Asperger's makes the situation even more so. Often times, we feel like pioneers, much like other parents must have felt in the early 1990's, when our country first began officially recognizing Asperger's Syndrome. Back then, the overwhelming population of boys diagnosed with the syndrome overshadowed the rest. Today, not much seems to have changed.

In many ways, I don't mind considering myself a pioneer. I always did like "Little House" books, written by Laura Ingalls Wilder, still like quilting, and being self-sufficient. As for Kristina, she loves the American Girl® series about Kirsten. And what girl doesn't want a horse?

Somehow, the real thing isn't as glamorous, is it? Especially when you are sitting in a covered wagon (Asperger's), while others (the school) swear it's just a minivan (wrong diagnosis). It gets even better when the doubters question the makers of the covered wagon (the doctors).

Sometimes, you just want to bang your head against a wall.

Or pull your hair out.

Except for me. I'd rather have gray hair than no hair.

For us, it's as if the doubters have locked into one understanding of Asperger's, solely in relation to boys.

Since Kristina does not match up exactly to that portrait, she "must" be misdiagnosed. Simply put, due to lack of experience with girls on the spectrum, their understanding is skewed. And that is not a good thing. See, I was there too. I had my own thoughts on the matter. Early on, I had my own view of autism.

When I closed my eyes and pictured autism, I imagined individuals who appeared physically different, who could not communicate like everyone else, if at all. I pictured individuals always needing help functioning in the day-to-day world, never experiencing life in the mainstream.

Then I had Kristina.

Kristina is our only daughter, our only child. As with other parents who have only one child, whatever is normal for Kristina is normal for us. There weren't any siblings to "compare" her to, nor were there any cousins or neighboring children her age. As a result, opportunities for social interaction with peers were sparse, existing for only a few minutes each week during Sunday School. Although her Sunday School class consisted of several girls her age, she never seemed to click with any of them. So it was hard to say which of her behaviors were normal, advanced, slow, or peculiar. All we knew was that Kristina is Kristina. Still, observing other parents with their children, whether at the store, or church, some of my daughter's behaviors seemed a bit, well, different.

As an infant, she was never much of a cuddler. She was not a baby you could rock to sleep—ever. The only times she wanted to be held was when she was sick. In fact, that became a flag for us. If Kristina wanted to be cuddled and held, we knew she wasn't feeling well. Though disappointed that she did not like cuddles and hugs, we did not think too much about it. After all, my husband and I are not huggers, either. We simply figured it was how she was.

I remember early on having to guard Kristina more closely than other kids her age appeared to need safeguarding. I had observed other kids her age who were largely able to stop when called to, or who seemed to have an innate sense of personal space, but Kristina did her own thing. I remember unending calls of caution as she would toddle down the driveway toward the street. I remember how my cries seemed to fall on deaf ears. I always had to be within an arm's reach of her to stop her from venturing out into the road. Kristina simply did not seem to have any sense of personal space.

Too late, I learned about dogs used as therapeutic means for kids like Kristina. In those days, I often wonder if a Border Collie might have been of help, nudging her back into the yard, or wherever else she needed to be.

Inside, it was not abnormal for Kristina to make her way from point A to point B, stepping on whatever was in her path—including people. More times than not, Kristina would trudge through the room, successfully arriving at her destination, totally oblivious to what had just happened. Not only did we repeatedly stop Kristina, pointing out the fact that she stepped on someone, we also had to teach her that was not a good thing. On top of that, she needed to learn that when she hears someone call out in pain, she needs to see if he is okay.

(Over time, we taught her to use the phrases "Are you okay? Is there anything I can do for you?" any time she heard someone say "ow." In practice, it works, but still comes off as rather scripted, which I suppose it is. To this day, a loud cry of pain or a simple "ouch" solicits an equal level of animated attention.)

Outside the home, there were other clues. Shopping was a constant mixture of filling the cart while redirecting Kristina from obliviously crossing the paths of other shoppers. Thank goodness, Kristina preferred riding in the cart. Even so, many trips ended with Kristina "losing it" in one way or another, usually via loud complaining or crying. At the mall, it proved near impossible to let our daughter walk alongside without holding her hand. She never seemed to "follow" where we were, constantly losing track of her surroundings.

As for behavior modification, we tried all sorts of things. Efforts at using reverse psychology proved transparent. Kristina was the first kid I ever ran across who never fell for it.

Not even once.

Kristina spoke early, and had a large vocabulary by age two. This was something else we passed off as insignificant. To us, it seemed perfectly normal. To her pediatrician, it seemed advanced. Maybe it's different for girls than boys when it comes to language delay and Asperger's. Regardless, Kristina spoke early, and well.

For Kristina, language delay did not apply.

Kristina spoke incessantly.

Kristina took to talking early; she is quite "oral." Her mouth is always going—whether something's going in it or on it, or sounds are coming out of it. She loves the feel of her special blanket pressed up against her lips. At school, her silky blonde hair is often twisted, and held to her mouth. When she was a baby, she preferred the sensation of the silky tags (belonging to her stuffed toys) in her mouth over the feel of their soft fur on her hands.

Thankfully, the "tag habit" was short-lived.

However, as soon as she discovered scissors, she chopped them all off.

Fortunately, I discovered her new hobby before she gave her Beanie Babies® a trim, and quickly found them a new home on a wooden shelf, out of Kristina's reach.

Kristina was also an early reader. I often wonder if her oral stimulation behavior played a role in her early reading capability. I wonder if her desire for constant oral stimulation, coupled with the enjoyment of producing sound, contributed to those early linguistic abilities. It is not a scientific hypothesis I present, but a simple observation and supposition. By early, I mean this: Kristina taught herself to read before she turned four. She learned to read by teaching herself.

More than once, we have had people assure us that we are duping ourselves. They swear it is impossible for a child that young to read anything. "It's pure memorization," they attested. Let's face it, most people thought we were simply exaggerating, and bragging. But my husband and I strongly disagree. Kristina was reading complete books by three-and-a-half years old. She read *Arthur's Birthday Party* by Lillian Hoban to my sister at three years and eight months. She wasn't coached, and only missed the word "somersault," (*Arthur's Birthday Party* is a Level 2 reader.)

It's funny how such great accomplishments are often questioned, rather than lauded. While talking to another family member, who was doing her best to wake me up from my fantasy of having an early reader, I pointed out one of the best pieces of proof for our case. When Kristina read, she often mispronounced words. If she was using her photographic memory, I doubt she would consistently do such. She pronounced words as anyone else learning would—by sounding them out. For example, when she saw the word "jumped" on a page, she would pronounce it "jump-ed", not "jumpt." One of our favorites is the word "youth," which she perpetually pronounced "yowth." After all, if "mouth" is "mowth," then isn't "youth" "yowth"?

Kristina's early reading opened my eyes to our own language. It's easy to take reading and pronunciation for granted when you've been at it for years. It's often hard to understand those who struggle with something that's so easy for you. But listening to her read aloud made the difficulty others have of learning our English language makes sense. It made me more empathetic.

Not too long ago, our family watched video clips from Kristina's youngest years. One in particular caught our attention. It was Kristina's third birthday, and she was quite excited. A few kids were coming over for a brief celebration, and Kristina couldn't wait. She sat at the decorated table, surrounded by paper plates and balloons. She grabbed a party blower, and played with it while the tape rolled. As I asked her about the day, Kristina communicated her excitement, all the while looking away from both the camera and me. It was quite obvious Kristina was avoiding eye contact (one of the markers of Asperger's Syndrome). All these years, I knew Kristina avoids such, but seeing it on camera, at such a young age, was revealing. Before we knew something was different enough to warrant further investigation, the markers were indeed there.

At home, Kristina preferred to play by herself. I would often check in on her, but she largely wanted to be alone. When we did play together, it was more "side by side" than interactive, regardless of my efforts.

Kristina never seemed lonely.

My daughter's playtime was limited in its themes, focusing primarily on birthdays (of her stuffed animals), shopping, and going to the doctor. Every day, there would be at least one birthday celebration. Most days, a doctor visit. Her play appeared to mimic life. Instead of pretending her animals were taking an imaginary trip to some far-off castle for a party, they celebrated each and every birthday just as Kristina had experienced them in her own life. She had specific props that she used, and a specific order she followed for each celebration. Doctor-play followed a similar route, as did grocery shopping.

As for playmates, the social world has never been an easy one for Kristina to maneuver in. Sunday School proved increasingly problematic for her. I recall one occasion when a little girl proudly declared to Kristina (in front of me) that she was "inviting everyone to my birthday party—except *you*!"

So much for the spirit of Christian Fellowship, huh?

Her limited interactions with other children, coupled with her inadequate responses to them, had us longing for more social opportunities. Perhaps her poor social behavior was merely a lack of little girls to play with, right?

As Kristina neared her fourth birthday, we were quite excited for her to begin preschool. Finally, she would meet some new kids, and have another opportunity to make some friends. Hopefully, she would have some play dates.

But life took another turn.

Downhill.

On bald tires.

As Kristina grew, the envisioned joys and laughter of preschool were replaced with dire concerns of her teacher. As other moms were greeted with bright smiles, I was routinely greeted with a worry line. More than once, I was called up, or called in for a meeting myself, to discuss Kristina's progress.

Kristina joined this particular preschool along with a few other children we knew. Surely, she interacted with them? Not exactly. In fact, Kristina did not seem to get along with anyone, and was causing a mite of trouble.

The teacher told us of the trouble she had directing Kristina's attention toward other activities. The slide was about the only thing Kristina wanted to be involved with. She showed little interest, if any, in playing with the other children. In fact, her teacher commented that Kristina did not get along well with the other kids.

The news got even better.

The teacher went on to say that when she spoke with Kristina about her actions, it was as if she wasn't there, or did not care. Kristina never looked at the teacher when she talked to her, seeming to stare beyond her when spoken to, causing concern that Kristina wasn't taking her seriously. This had the teacher so troubled, she conveyed to me her worry that Kristina just might be on the road to becoming a juvenile delinquent.

Sadly, I'm not exaggerating. The teacher appeared quite serious in her concern and prediction. She really did mention that she felt if Kristina did not change, she would probably wind up in juvenile hall.

I can only imagine what she thought of our household. We knew Kristina had trouble relating with other kids, but juvenile hall seemed a bit much of a prediction for a three-and-a-half year old. I offered to add Kristina to another day, but the teacher's eyes opened wide, as she ran her fingers through her curly red hair, quickly uttering something along the lines of, "No!"

I was a bit taken aback. After all, Kristina seemed to struggle socially, so maybe she needed more time interacting with kids, right?

Wrong.

At least not on Mrs. Preschool's clock.

We didn't know what to do.

I wonder what her teacher would have thought if Kristina was a Caleb. I wonder if she would have seen an active boy who borders on being a bully. I wonder if she would have been frustrated, but not to the point of despair. I wonder if the year would have flowed smoother.

Looking back, the preschool was a mistake all around. Other than snack time, it offered no structure, something Kristina sorely needed, and still does. Live and learn.

Life has a way of hurtling by, and before we knew it, Kristina was headed to the big time. She was going to elementary school. At every opportunity, I asked parents their opinions on our neighborhood school. After the disappointing experience with the preschool, we wanted to make sure our daughter was headed to an excellent place. Regardless of personality, religion, or social position, everyone spoke positively about it. We were encouraged.

Besides, a good public school beats paying tuition.

Though typically anxious, like other new parents, we were excited about this new phase of her life. All too soon, a big yellow bus would come and take our daughter to an unfamiliar brick building, only a few blocks away, leaving me standing alone in the driveway, eyes full of tears.

But before that could happen, we needed to attend Kindergarten orientation.

We began our meeting in the school's warm library, sitting on small wooden chairs. After a brief introduction, our children left for their own get-acquainted session. Shortly thereafter, we made our way down to the Kindergarten classroom. There, the reading teacher stopped by to speak with us. As she spoke on goals, curriculum, and such, all I could think of was how bored Kristina was going to be. Afterwards, I spoke privately to the woman, mentioning to her that Kristina was already reading. Her body language appeared to convey she didn't believe Kristina could read more than "cat, "hat," and her own name. I chuckled to myself, and didn't push the issue. She'll find out for herself, I thought.

(In fact, when Kristina was tested during first grade, the results revealed that Kristina was reading at an eighth-grade level. Yes, her comprehension was not at the same level [it was somewhere near a third-grade level], but she could *read* the words, just the same. She did, indeed, understand much of what she read.)

Sometimes parents do live in a bubble of disbelief or denial. Sometimes, however, parents have correctly assessed their child's abilities.

It wasn't until elementary school that a picture started to emerge. Even with a solid structure now in place, Kristina still had difficulty.

Somewhere along the way, some time after Kristina the Kindergartner turned five, we developed a sneaking suspicion there was more to Kristina than your ordinary, immature child. It was as if the social behaviors were a sneeze, the early reading was a rash, and the repetitive play was watery eyes. On their own, they may not amount to much, but together, they were cause for concern. As the physical symptoms in the illustration point to allergies, Kristina's pointed toward autism. As with allergies, it took a while for a specific diagnosis to come clear.

Kristina seemed to have overwhelming anxiety concerning the videos played in the classroom. If the teacher chose to turn out the lights for the flick, all bets were off. Kristina would cry, cover her ears, and verbally protest.

Then there was the "b" word.

It rhymes with "mutton."

At arts-and-crafts time, Kristina refused to touch anything with a button on it. All her snowmen were created sans buttons. If a button even grazed her skin, she would screech, let out a stream of verbal complaints, and do her level best to wipe the area it touched "clean." We discussed this idiosyncrasy with her Kindergarten teacher, and she did not seem too concerned. We figured her button aversion was due to quirkiness, and would resolve in time.

It soon became painfully obvious that Kristina was standing apart from her peers. Most girls left her out of their play, both at school and church. She did manage some play dates, the successes of which were spotty. Like all other girls in her class, she was included in the "invite everyone" birthday parties. However, she seemed unable to "click" with any of those girls.

Kindergarten came and went. I, for one, was very thankful it was only a half-day program. Kristina's teacher seemed firm, funny, and fair. To me, she did not come across as a stereotypical Kindergarten teacher, full of fluff, ruffles, and sunbeams, but she was exactly the kind of teacher Kristina needed for her first year in school.

And Kristina loved her.

Overall, her teacher did not seem too worried about Kristina's behavior. Communications from her lacked the perceived unease and pessimism of Mrs. Preschool, so we were not too concerned. We chalked it all up to personality, and immaturity, nothing more.

Quite frankly, the lack of friends and play dates bothered us much more than it bothered Kristina.

By the time first grade rolled around, we were certain there was increasingly more to Kristina than we had earlier suspected. We knew there was more to it than a bright child with a willful personality, in dire need of social graces. We knew *something* was different; but we had no idea what. The harsh words of the preschool teacher lingered in my head, and I knew she was wrong. However, I also knew something wasn't quite "right," too.

Still, first grade started much like Kindergarten, with little, if any, negative communication from her teacher indicating that anything substantial was amiss.

Then, a few months into the school year, we got "the call."

The kind that parents of little girls in first grade are not supposed to get.

The one where the teacher let us know there was a problem.

With *our* child.

Kristina's teacher informed us that Kristina had quite a bit of trouble adjusting to first grade. She initially thought it was simply the transition to a full day at school, but her difficulties were not waning. She went on to provide specifics, most of which revolved around Kristina's classroom behavior. Kristina had great difficulty transitioning from subject to subject. She burst into tears, covering her ears anytime there was a video, storm, or assembly. She did not display respect for teachers, or others in authority. She had no compunction speaking her mind to adults, and could be very argumentative. (Ironically, Ms. First Grade admitted that, although her behavior was unacceptable, she was almost always right when it came to confronting/correcting those adults.)

Kristina was also very bright, and Ms. First Grade had a very hard time keeping her busy, while the others kids took a much longer time completing worksheets. She kept running out of extra worksheets and coloring pages to give her.

In brief, Kristina was a handful.

Several weeks of blissful quiet from the school, followed by a wealth of negative information appearing seemingly out of nowhere, was numbing. We felt blindsided. Suddenly, the sensation of ice water spewing onto our heads, down our backs seemed almost real. The initial shock of cold led to a lingering, uncomfortable dampness in my heart, like heavy jeans after a long walk through mountains of snow.

Kristina was having trouble. Kristina was trouble. Kristina had been trouble—for weeks.

We did the only thing we could think of at the time. We tried to get to the bottom of it. We asked a bunch of questions. We asked for the teacher's insight. We asked why she waited so long to fill us in. We asked what we could do to support her. We did our best to listen with an open mind. In some way, the call ended.

I cried.

We cried.

I felt like a failure as a parent.

Andrew and I sat down, letting it all sink in, in our own ways. We analyzed the call, the facts, and the potential ramifications. It was as if a trap door had suddenly opened beneath our feet, sending us hurtling in the cool darkness to some unknown destination. *This is the time to cling to each other. This is the time to pull together, not drift apart. This is the time to work as a team. We have to stay connected. It is okay to cry, but keep moving, even though the darkness is overwhelming. Keep focused on Kristina.*

Adversity can build up or tear down. Andrew and I knew that we needed to rely on each other to travel successfully down whichever path lay ahead. Still, it was tough. It did not matter whether or not we were ready for this unexpected journey; we had to head out, just the same. Our only choices were to either move along willingly, faces forward, or be dragged, looking anywhere but ahead.

One day, shortly after the phone call, Andrew had lunch with a friend of his. As with most friends who get together, their small talk ultimately turned toward the kids, and Andrew shared some concerns we were having with Kristina. Many of the stories his friend recounted about his son resembled ours. At that point, Bill took a chance, and introduced Andrew to something his son had: Asperger's. At the time, we didn't know anything about it, including how to spell it, let alone the formal name: Asperger's Syndrome Disorder. Bill gently encouraged Andrew to read up on it, trying not to push Andrew into presuming it applied to Kristina.

Once home, Andrew began to research Asperger's Syndrome Disorder. What he found resonated with us: strict adherence to routine, resistance to transitions, intense interests in only a few subjects, social struggles. The struggles over the past few years were starting to make sense. For the first time, we could see an image forming through the fog. Slowly, the blinders were starting to lift, giving us for the first time a glimpse of what was going on with our daughter. The pieces of the puzzle were starting to fall into place. Difficulties with her peers, the trouble shifting between tasks, her obsession with birthdays and birthday parties, and the ever present sense that she was not always "with us"—all flashed before our minds. We truly believed we were on to something. Pointed to the right path, we could feel our spirits lifting. Soon, we would have the combination to unlocking Kristina.

And it would not be "poor parenting" greeting us at the end of this expedition.

A flicker of light piercing the darkness gives such a lift to the spirit.

In order to move forward, we needed affirmation or rejection of our newfound supposition—we needed to know if we were right. We immediately made an appointment to speak with Kristina's pediatrician.

Her pediatrician did not seem surprised at all when we told her we thought something was up with Kristina. In fact, she seemed to have a pretty good idea. She was cautious with her wording, mentioning Pervasive Developmental Disorder, "PDD," as her initial diagnosis. We didn't really know what that meant at the time. At home, we discovered it is a term for an unspecified diagnosis, typically including elements of autism. Her pediatrician recommended we look into testing provided by the school, and consider making an appointment with a highly respected Developmental Services Center, located in the local teaching hospital.

Meanwhile, her pediatrician recommended using earplugs for noisy situations, such as assemblies and school videos. By chance, we just happened to acquire some simple earplugs from a tour at Andrew's company. We were set. We spoke with her teacher, and she agreed to keep them in the classroom for those times when Kristina's sensitivity to sound flared up.

In the meantime, the school continued to raise concerns, throwing more ice water upon us, requesting testing for Kristina themselves. The school appeared to have its own assumptions as to the root of her struggles, and they were quite different from Kristina's doctor's assumptions.

As we later learned, the diagnostic process varies from case to case. As can be imagined, healthcare coverage, as well as the school's own policies (and budgets) determine the particular road map for each individual. In our case, the school played an integral part in the diagnostic process.

Our school district's procedure was for the school to administer all the applicable testing it could before sending Kristina off-site for additional testing. If the school deemed she needed a deeper, more thorough assessment than the school could provide, the school would find it and fund it. We were aware that the school would not be able to give her a medical diagnosis, and, along with the school, were certain she needed one. Still, procedure had to be followed before referring her to the Developmental Services Center. One thing led to another, and with the help of Kristina's very talented and gifted pediatrician, we were able to work with the school, acquiring timely and needed testing for Kristina.

At the end of the day, we were a muddled mix of excitement, anxiety, pessimism, and optimism. Even

Asperger's in Pink

with the paperwork underway, a full tank of gas, and a clear blue sky, the road to Developmental Services Center proved more of a Sunday drive than a highway run.

First stop: Elementary School, Testing, and Evaluations.

PINK PEARLS
for Chapter One

FOR THE CAREGIVERS

· ·

Dogs just might do the trick

There is positive discussion regarding the use of thera-peutic dogs for children on the autism spectrum. Depending on your family situation (time, finances—and allergies), they may be a welcome addition.

Meet and speak

If things seem off, make appointments with appropriate personnel. Are there issues at school? Speak with the teacher. Is there a deeper suspicion there is an underly-ing cause to the difficulties? Speak with your child's pediatrician (without the child present, of course.) Allow yourself to be open to discussing your child with the professionals in her life.

Asperger's in Pink

Learn the ropes

Be proactive in acquiring knowledge regarding testing and the testing process. Do not assume the roadmap will be given to you without your request. Don't be afraid to ask questions about the process.

Keep it level

If concerns arise, resist the urge to be defensive or confrontational. Listen—even if you disagree—truly listen to those around you, taking time to hear what they are saying.

FOR OTHERS

Speak (up) in love

Let the parents know of any concerns, and do so in a timely manner. Try not to make any assumptions, but be honest when speaking with the parents.

Be a pointer

Do you know the next step the parents should take? Point them in the best direction, and provide them with appropriate contact information, as well as any expectations or responsibilities.

A cup is better than a bucket

Be judicious in the timing and amount of difficult information you must provide to the caregivers regarding their child. Negative information is always hard to swallow, but a bucketful can nearly choke you. If problems arise early on, choose not to let them pile up before informing the caregivers.

I AM THANKFUL FOR...

. . . .

Kristina's pediatrician who was with us from day one, looking—objectively and wisely—for the best interests of our daughter.

INSIDE the
BUBBLE

DON'T Take Me Out to the Ball Game!

Slowly and carefully, our sedan pulled into the stadium's small parking lot. Andrew chose a spot near the back, hoping to avoid foul-ball territory. Gathering our jackets and caps, we made our way to the ticket counter as Kristina scowled. It was bad enough that we had disrupted her predictable Friday night routine. Taking her to the ballpark added insult to injury.

"I just know they are going to have fireworks!" worried Kristina. "It's going to be so loud!"

One bad experience watching major league ball trumped a handful of good ones at the minors. The fact that fireworks were not on the schedule was irrelevant. The reality of a loud, fireworks-saturated game, three years prior, cemented the possibility that we, and the ballpark's schedule, could be wrong. To Kristina, that was all that mattered.

"Do you want to give your own ticket to the lady at the gate?" asked Andrew, offering a red one to Kristina.

Kristina's blonde hair fluttered in the breeze. Her gaze remained frustrated and unyielding.

"I guess," she muttered, taking it with her small hand.

"Good evening, folks!" greeted the ticket taker. "How are you doing tonight?" the kind woman asked, looking toward Kristina.

Kristina simply handed her the red ticket, looking toward the paved ground, and slowly moved herself away from the woman, never saying a word, or even acknowledging her. Andrew and I exchanged greetings, handed her our tickets, and headed in to find seats.

"Maybe this was a bad idea," said Andrew, looking sideways at me.

"You know she will be fine once we are here for a few innings," I said. "She always is."

Both Andrew and I knew that Kristina would settle in at some point during the evening. But getting there was always a challenge.

This small stadium has provided a nice training ground for Kristina to stretch herself. The stands are simple. General Admission tickets allow fans to pick and choose any seat they like within the bleachers. The game itself, low minor leagues—but we don't mind. Truth be told, I don't follow baseball. Not much, anyway. For me, the pace of the stadium has always been somewhat cathartic.

Slow, relaxed, and quaint. Seeing the sun sink behind left field, leaving gold and orange along the way, provides such a calming effect. The fact that there is plenty of space for Kristina to move around also gives freedom.

Most fans come from the surrounding rural area. Young teens, and even some preteens, barely watch the game, congregating instead behind the stands, sitting at a few scattered tables. Some prefer to saunter aimlessly up and down the walkway between the stands and the Box Seats, forever talking into cell phones or dipping into fried food.

But those who do come for the game itself are devoted and rustic. This is farm country, in many ways, far from the buses and cabs of Lower Manhattan, and far removed in time, as well. Men in overalls sit under John Deere caps, cheering on the young men in the field. Women, faces worn by the summer sun and time, cheer along, leaving fashion to the wandering teens.

The relaxed feel of this ballpark suits our family just fine.

"Why do we have to sit here?" questioned Kristina, as we found some spots a little to the left of home plate.

"We want to sit behind the net in case a ball heads to the stands," said my husband, giving me an exasperated look, as if to say, "Remind me why we are doing this."

"Kristina, just sit, please," I begged, dusting the seat off with a napkin.

"I'm sitting between you and Daddy."

And with that, Kristina plopped down on the bench, stuck her elbows to the side, and covered her ears with the palms of her hands.

"There's not a lot of noise, Kristina."

"I don't care. There will be."

"They have to play the National Anthem before the game starts," reminded Andrew.

Kristina looked up at her father for a brief moment, and then laid her head on his lap, her ears still covered, and elbows still protruding.

"When can we go home, Mommy?" shot up the small voice.

"Honey, the game hasn't even started yet. Please put your hands down."

"But what time can we go home? How about 7:30."

It was only 6:57 p.m.

"Kristina, you're shouting."

"I am not!"

"Yes, you are."

"But I can't hear myself."

"That's because you have your ears covered. One hand down, Kristina," I pleaded, using hand motions as well as words to get the message across.

Reluctantly, Kristina moved her hand slightly off her ear.

"So we're going home at 7:30, right?"

"I didn't say that."

"But you said we weren't going to stay for the entire game."

"Yes, but the game doesn't even start until 7:05."

"The speakers are loud, Mommy. Why do we have to sit here?"

"Actually, the speakers aren't too bad here. See," I said, pointing to small, black boxes dotted throughout the stands, "they are all over. I have your earplugs, if you want them."

"Okay, I guess," said Kristina, reluctantly holding her palm open for the blue and yellow plugs. Who knew something so simple as these earplugs, could be so helpful.

"They're starting the National Anthem," cut in Andrew, "We all need to stand up, and not talk during it. You need to stand, Kristina."

Thankfully, Kristina complied.

Looking toward the field, a young woman in a purple wrap shirt stood, ready to sing. The few souls in the stands joined in, as all stood in the direction of the flag out in right field, the glare of the sun making it difficult to find.

Sometimes it seemed as if we would never be able to up and go anywhere without some resistance from Kristina. It didn't matter where we suggested, or what we might do—but you could bet the house that Kristina would object. I think it all boils down to control. One thing that helps Kristina stay afloat in this world is the sense of stability she gets from her everyday routine. In Kristina's world, one small change, such as a last minute trip to the store, might as well be a change in the Prime Directive.

The trouble is that Kristina has to function in this world. And this world doesn't seem to take the time to understand, or even fully accept, kids like Kristina.

For now, I try not to wonder what the fans sitting above us are pondering about this young girl, who is visibly upset about being at the ballgame. No one has said anything, though a few have openly gazed in our direction. One gentleman in particular shot us a disapproving look. I muster a weak smile in Andrew's direction, and we both sigh.

"I see the mascot!" yelled Kristina, shooting up straight in her seat. "Can we go see him, Daddy? Can we go down there now?"

As quickly as that, the spell is broken, and the night again appears calm and cool. Smiles and laughter replace Kristina's tears and anxiety. Once the team's mascot came into view, it was as if nothing happened. Andrew and Kristina worked on keeping score. I worked on relaxing as I sat, wondering if I should have brought my knitting, like the older woman a few rows back.

This is such an oasis from day-to-day living. Not too far, but far enough away from home to feel as though we've left town for a bit. And I need that sometimes. And I need it tonight.

Before too long, darkness has fallen, and nine bells have sounded. Time to pack up and head home. I take the pencil from Andrew, placing it back into my purse. Kristina has a bounce in her step as we pass by groups of kids throwing balls and giggling non-stop in the concourse.

I pause and wonder if Kristina will someday be invited to join in with kids like that. Will she be part of a giggling group of tweens? Will she have the wherewithal to be left with her friends to roam around a ballpark?

Will she even be given a chance?

Andrew takes the back roads home, keeping the relaxed pace of the evening with us.

Kristina made it tonight, and we're all stronger because of it.

Chapter Two

It's a Girl ...
with Asperger's!

Waiting outside for the bus, on a cold winter's day:

"Kristina, put your hood up."

"Why?"

"It's 17 degrees outside."

"Mommy, I don't need to cover up my hair. It can't feel anything."

— KRISTINA, AGE 9

Thankfully, we did not have to wait long for the on-site assessments to begin. Even with mounds of paperwork to take care of, the entire process flowed quickly. Kristina received several different types of testing, including a psychological evaluation, as well as IQ testing. At home, Andrew and I filled out all sorts of forms and questionnaires. Following the advice of a friend, I purchased a large binder, and filled it with copies of all submitted paperwork, as well as other pertinent forms. I also started a journal. All in all, the process took several weeks, which seemed reasonable.

Andrew and I still recall, as if it were yesterday, the meeting with the school psychologist. We scheduled the conference during the school day, in the psychologist's room. As we sat at a low wood-veneer table, on petite plastic chairs, the kind gentleman greeted us with wide-opened eyes. As we waited for him to begin the meeting, he commented how surprised he was that we both made the meeting. Andrew and I were confused, not sure what to make of his comments, or facial expression. We asked if we had the right day. He answered that we did, again mentioning his surprise. Finally, one of us spoke up.

"Don't both parents always make these meetings?"

He answered, "No," telling us that typically only one parent shows, and, sometimes, neither show up at all. He went on to say how unusual it was, in his experience, for both to attend such meetings. We were quite surprised. No wonder we suspected the school was scrutinizing us. We were an anomaly.

We felt that showing up in tandem only helped to demonstrate how sincere we were in helping our daughter. Even if we hadn't felt that way, we would have still attended the meeting together, as a team. It boggled our minds that the majority of parents did not do the same.

With that, we began our meeting.

The results were positive, affirming our suspicions all along that Kristina was a strong reader, among a few other things. As the school and her pediatrician suspected, they did indeed show Kristina needed further testing, which the school could not provide, but deemed essential. At that point, the school officially recommended and referred Kristina to the Developmental Services Center.

We were on our way.

As the school did the referring, the school also took care of the cost. I cannot overstate how grateful we are that the school provided the testing at the Center for Kristina. Like many other parents, we would have found it difficult to pay for all the needed testing ourselves. We live a simple life. The only nanny ever to grace our home resides on the cover of a DVD.

Obtaining an appointment at the Center took several months. Thankfully, a few of the professionals clued us in ahead of time, so we were aware of the backlog. As both the school and pediatrician seemed certain Kristina would need to go through the Center, and all desired the results sooner than later, we made the appointment as soon as feasible.

After much discussion and prayer, we opted not to inform extended family of Kristina's testing before it occurred. With all of our family living out of the area, we frankly did not see any benefit in involving them in the initial conversation. After all, there was always the possibility that everything would come back either negative or inconclusive. We did not want anyone to worry.

Nor did we want our own stress levels increased.

At the heart of it all, we are very private people, and this was a very private matter. We never have regretted that decision. It didn't help that a few had already criticized our parenting on more than one occasion—in front of Kristina, even.

After years of wondering, and months of waiting, the day of the testing at the Developmental Services Center arrived. The appointment lasted a half day, and was very thorough. Both a physician and an educator examined Kristina. We really liked this approach, as Kristina was observed by two people from different disciplines. We felt it allowed for a more objective diagnosis. Andrew and I were also part of the process, interviewed thoroughly. The professionals asked all sorts of questions, including family histories, an eclectic mix about my pregnancy, including Kristina's birth itself.

The interview was so thorough, I half wondered if they'd ask if I slept facing the moon while pregnant.

We waited for hours while they completed the process with Kristina. After the team made their conclusions, we placed Kristina in an on-site childcare room, just a few doors away. Such a setup made it possible for both of us to meet with them. For us, obtaining a daytime babysitter was not a realistic option, as our sitters were high school students.

Thankfully, we did not have to wait weeks for a stilted diagnosis, chock-full of terminology and suggestions in need of a translator—delivered via a large manila envelope. We received all of the initial information regarding Kristina right there, on the spot, and were able to ask all sorts of questions about it.

The results of the team echoed comments her pediatrician had made earlier in the year. It also confirmed our suspicions. During the diagnostic process, the honest answers spewing from my lips seemed to fit into descriptors we had previously read regarding Asperger's

Syndrome, making me concerned that I had inadvertently skewed the results. But that was not the case at all.

In fact, I recall the doctor mentioning that we should not feel we did anything to slant the diagnosis towards Asperger's.

It was if he read my mind. He went on to describe test results, and their observations apart from our initial verbal input, in support of their conclusions. However, it was also as if he was saying to us: *Relax. This diagnosis is firm, and you can have faith in it. You did nothing to manipulate this diagnosis.* We were simply attuned to the possibility, more so than other parents were.

So it was, during the middle of first grade, at age six, Kristina was officially diagnosed with Asperger's Syndrome Disorder.

The combination lock opened, the fog lifted, darkness no longer enveloped us. We could finally see Kristina for who she is, who God created her to be. Bill was right. Her pediatrician was right. Now we had it in black and white, signed, soon to be sealed, and delivered—via a large manila envelope. We left for home knowing what we needed to know to help Kristina grow. It was a very caring experience.

Once we had the official diagnosis, we were a bit relieved. Months of paperwork, filling out forms, and a myriad of testing leading to a diagnosis were finally over. At last, we knew what we were working with. We had papers from credible people to back us up.

We weren't nuts.

We felt exonerated.

Kristina was, simply, Kristina.

But we didn't open up a bottle of champagne and dance around the house, either. Later on at home, when Kristina was off to sleep, we sat down on our couch, and cried.

It's often said that not knowing is worse than knowing. The fear of the unknown often supersedes the fear you can touch. Finally, we knew. Kristina, indeed, was super special. She was atypical. Kristina has an Autism Spectrum Disorder. For real. This wasn't a result of our parenting style, or how I slept when I was pregnant. In short, we didn't "do" anything "wrong."

Still, the relief of having a valid diagnosis was quickly overrun by the realization of the diagnosis itself. Along with it came new anxieties and concerns. Would she be able to make long and lasting friendships? Would she stay in a mainstream school setting? Would she be able to live on her own some day? Have a family of her own? And what about family? How are they going to respond to this? What does the road ahead look like for us? What do we do next?

It was all so overwhelming. It also meant that Kristina's road would probably have more hills, curves, and bumps than the road many other kids in her class would have. This was a hard reality to take.

Once again, the unknown conquered the known. It was a hard day.

It's an odd thing to cry over something that isn't taking your child's life away. After all, we were told she had Asperger's Syndrome. Her prognosis, if you will, was very positive. Still, when we considered the struggles she would face compared to her peers, it was a tough road to mull over. It was also evidence that Kristina is, and will forever be, just a bit different.

It took months, from beginning to end, to have the diagnosis in hand. From everything we read, and from what we were told, the fact that she was diagnosed at age six seemed early, especially for girls. We felt very fortunate.

We knew we would need to let extended family know, but wanted to make sure *we* fully understood Asperger's Syndrome Disorder before contacting anyone. As we made each phone call, we did our best to explain Asperger's. Early on, we found that this isn't as easy to explain as your average condition, like hay fever.

"She doesn't seem autistic to *me*," was a common response. A non-enthusiastic, "Oh," was another. Others asked when she would be "cured."

We mailed copies of bits and pieces of information to the grandparents, hoping to help them understand Asperger's. We gave website addresses, book titles, and so on to the rest.

Telling our circle of friends was a harder call. We shared the news as we saw fit. The reactions varied. Unfortunately, all but Andrew's friend were unfamiliar with Asperger's Syndrome.

Suddenly, we found ourselves in the position of educator and ambassador for Asperger's Syndrome Disorder. As time has gone by, we continue to hone those important roles, still having much to learn.

Meanwhile, Andrew and I had to decide where to go next. We were given different options, from looking into social skills groups to school support. We had psychologists to consider. We also had more reading to do than could be done over any given weekend. There was a lot on our plate, and we were still stuffed from the diagnostic meeting.

As for Kristina, we spoke with her briefly about the diagnosis. Truth be told, although bright, Kristina was still fairly young. We simplified the fancy, complex language into a few simple sentences. We started by encouraging her, affirming that she was bright.

Kristina, being Kristina, concurred.

We reminded her that some children struggled in school, though she found it easy. Kristina was more than willing to provide names to back up that particular statement. To Kristina, she was simply pointing out facts. To others, it would sound more like arrogance. We paused the discussion, reminding Kristina that we all have struggles.

Back on track, we taught her that some kids have a difficult time in school, but make friends easily. Some kids have it pretty easy with school, but making friends can be tough, while yet other kids have a hard (or easy) time with both. We told her that although she does great in school, she needed a little more help making friends. As she could picture classmates who fit each description, this method seemed to work okay. It was also as far as we went at the time.

I have to admit, somewhere, in the dark recesses of my mind, telling a child she has "Asperger's," knowing that she'd have no compunction sharing it with those around her, had me concerned.

Although overwhelmed with the road that lay ahead, relief was at hand. We knew what we were looking for, even if unable to find it right away. Meanwhile, we researched, read, and researched some more. We did the best we could to understand Asperger's. It was a lot to take in.

We learned that in spite of the fact that a Viennese physician, Hans Asperger, shed first light on this syndrome in 1944, it was decades until such knowledge gained worldwide acceptance. We learned that the Diagnostic and Statistical Manual of Mental Disorders (DSM-IV) did not officially include Asperger's until 1994—fewer than ten years before Kristina's diagnosis. In light of that truth, we felt fortunate Kristina was diagnosed, at all.

We also felt uneasy.

To us, this newfound knowledge meant we would be lucky if the road ahead was a gravel road, let alone paved. Many had gone before us, though not enough to gain significant attention. At the time, information specifically regarding young girls and Asperger's was sparse, at best. Putting on pioneering caps, we loaded up the proverbial wagon, and have done our best to forge ahead ever since.

Our life path took a different turn than we ever envisioned. In many ways, it felt like other parents had simple, intact maps to follow, along with clear directions. We felt our map was a complex one, with a giant hole ripped out of the middle of it.

Every now and then, we are able to follow a well-worn trail. Other times, we find ourselves cutting away low hanging branches, and tall grasses as we create the way ourselves. Sometimes, the wagon simply breaks down, we have to step away from it all, and rejuvenate. At least we have a general direction to follow, as well as a basic supply list.

Next stop: Third Grade.

Supplies: Patience, Perseverance, and Prayer.

PINK PEARLS

for Chapter Two

FOR THE CAREGIVERS

Stamina is a good thing

The testing process alone can be draining, regardless of the results. Be prepared for a long journey, and take care of yourself along the way.

Binders are your friends

Purchase a large 3-ring binder, label it, and put it to use immediately. This is not the time to procrastinate. Considering all the necessary paperwork, make your mantra: "fill it out, make copies, file/send back, follow up."

Listen

Make sure to make the meetings. No matter the amount of research you have done, or how many questions you may have, *listen first* to the professionals during the diagnostic process.

Learn

Thankfully, autism and Asperger's are more widely discussed than even a decade ago. Finding sources for information, be it clinical or otherwise, is easy to do via the web or most local bookstores. Take advantage of the knowledge that is out there, and learn, trying not to overwhelm yourself. There will be plenty of time down the road to acquire exhaustive knowledge, if you want it. Don't ignore the situation. Take the time to truly understand your child's diagnosis. It also goes without saying that you should understand those who are testing your child; their general qualifications, and what they plan to do with the information once a diagnosis is made, or test results come back.

Leave

Leave the guilt on the shelf. Asperger's is not a result of something you, or your family, "did." Although it may feel as if your family is under a perpetual microscope, resist the desire to focus inward. Keep your focus on your child.

Love

Your child is your child is your child. Nothing will ever change that, nor should anything ever negatively affect the love you have for her.

It's all right to cry

Whether its time spent with a box of tissues or a staring blankly into space, take time to come to grips with the diagnosis in a *healthy* manner. The more time that expires between the diagnosis and your internal acknowledgement of it, the harder it will be when reality finally sinks in.

FOR THE PROFESSIONALS

Provide contacts

If there is an Asperger's/Autism Spectrum Disorder contact at the hospital, or through the school district, provide that information to the caregivers, so they can have an additional resource to talk to once the diagnosis is in hand.

Respect their stress

Keep in mind the fact that the caregivers may have no idea how the process works, or what lies around the bend. This can be an incredibly overwhelming time for them. Recognize their stress, and work with them in light of that.

Clarity is a good thing

Terms and procedures need to be carefully explained to the caregivers, be it the testing process, or where to go "from here." Simplicity is best, at first. Be reasonable in the time needed to provide accurate feedback to the caregivers.

Let them know when they should realistically receive testing results, as this will help lessen their anxiety.

On-site sitting!

If at all possible, provide on-site child care during the evaluation phase of the testing process, so that both caregivers may be present. It is very difficult for some families to acquire childcare during the school day or on week nights.

I AM THANKFUL FOR

. . . .

An early, solid as a rock diagnosis, by the patient, kind, thorough and sincere professionals who diagnosed Kristina with Asperger's, providing a much needed, unwavering foundation, lasting through this very day.

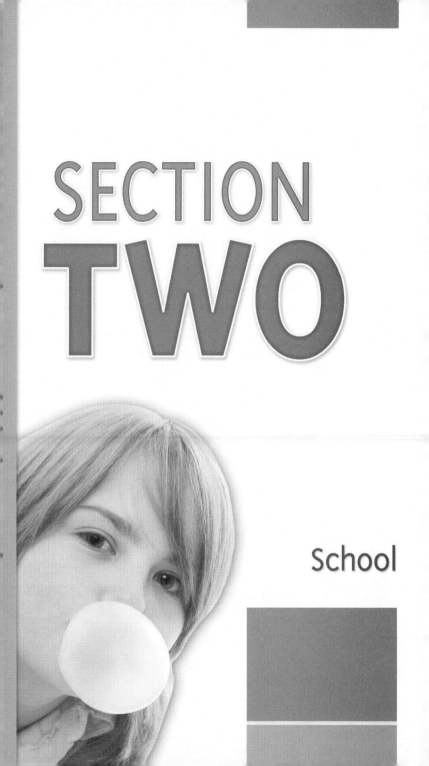

SECTION TWO

School

INSIDE the
BUBBLE

Misunderstanding the Rules

The January chill of this Tuesday morning shot through me like a thousand knives. If it weren't for the calm, bright summers, I'd lose my mind. Today was a classic, blustery, Great Lakes sort of day. Only twenty minutes left to get Kristina ready for school, yet my concentration was off.

Last night's e-mail from the teacher lingers in my mind. The assignment was to imagine teaching someone who had never made a snowball, to make one. As Kristina had never made one, herself, she wouldn't even pretend that she had. The e-mail detailed her frustration, which spilled over into the classroom.

How do I explain this one without sounding like a parent who is in denial of her child's behavior? All I could think of was what her teacher must be thinking of us. After all, what child living in snow country has never made her own snowball? Surely, he must think we keep her locked indoors all winter, chained in front of the television with a bowl full of chips. Somehow, I think he would be surprised to learn that snow fights (throwing handfuls of snow) are one of my daughter's favorite winter activities.

The truth is, Kristina has never successfully made a snowball. It's not for a lack of trying. It's not for a lack of teaching. She just has not "gotten it." Her gross motor skills are still developing. And right now, she just can't do it. End of story.

Okay, well, not the end. I still had to explain why Kristina refused to do the assignment. Kristina cannot pretend that she has made a snowball, when, in fact, she has not. To her, that would be lying. Off went a note to Mr. Wesley, another situation clarified.

I hope.

I thought raising girls meant less taxing communication between home and the school.

Silly me.

Only seventeen minutes to go, and I needed to help Kristina focus. Time to get my head out of last night's problem and on to today's solutions, such as getting Kristina ready for the bus.

"Aren't they going to cancel school today?" asked Kristina. I stood in the kitchen, glaring angrily toward the road. The temperature read one degree, with a wind chill of minus nineteen. The traffic reports stressed the need for those who don't need to be out to stay home, off the roads. It also was a bad time to be outside, for people with conditions like asthma, which Kristina has. Everywhere I looked, I saw cold, flaky white snow.

School was still on.

"But they said on the radio that you should stay home because it's so bad outside."

"I know, honey," I replied. "You have school today. I don't know why. It doesn't make sense to me. We need to get you ready."

Inside, I boiled like a volcano ready to break through the final layer of sediment and spew my molten frustration onto whoever it was who made the decision to send these children out in this cold onto slippery, dangerous roads. The mantra at election time is "educators are for the children, everything is for the children."

The apparent truth is the educators in this district seem to be all about the tests. This is testing week, and school will be held by candlelight if need be.

When I was young, school would have been canceled the night before. Other times, we made our way there, only to be returned home an hour later. And it wasn't anywhere near this cold or slippery out. This is something I have never gotten used to, and it is something I cannot explain as "normal" to my daughter.

Often our expectations of life form in our early years. To my husband and me, snow meant snow days, sleeping in, sledding and snowmen. It's as if that is the way it should be, and any deviation is against what is right and good. But Andrew and I now live in another part of the country than that of our early years.

When I was little, I dreamed of living in a place with a view that rivaled Santa's workshop. I often wondered what it would be like to drive on packed snow, surrounded by blankets of white. Here, snow is meant to be plowed, and shoveled. Now I simmer and curse the white slippery stuff, as I bundle my daughter up to head outside into the dangerous cold to hop on a bus for school.

Kristina often comes home with her hat off, and coat unzipped. No matter how often I remind her, or plead with her to come home all bundled up, she sporadically complies—or remembers. That type of behavior today may harm her. What adds to my worry is her lack of sensitivity to cold. Kristina simply does not notice cold like most people do. In fact, if it were up to Kristina, she would never wear gloves, as she seldom senses cold.

"Kristina, you have to remember to have your hood up and your coat zipped when you get off the bus today," I implored her.

The winds continued to howl, and the bus appeared only two minutes behind schedule. *Be thankful that she only has to walk down our drive-*

way. Be thankful she doesn't have to walk to a stop and wait. She will be fine. Relax. Stop worrying so much. Kristina is going to be perfectly fine. I have to work through this.

Thursday's weather was much like Tuesday's. My simmering turned into a boil, and I took a chance and called the school. If I decided to keep Kristina home, her absence would be considered illegal since the school deemed it okay to have school open. I hung up the phone, stifled a scream, cursed under my breath, and cried.

I was tempted to call and say she was sick. I knew that would be a lie, and I didn't want to lie. I also knew that if I tried that, Kristina would go to school the next day and inform everyone that she was not sick, and only stayed home because I was mad at the school for not closing.

Kristina equals full disclosure.

I called Andrew up, who assured me I was worrying a bit much. He pointed out the obvious, that she had a quick trip on and off the bus.

He was right. I needed to take a cue from the weather, and cool off.

The day ended with another letter from her teacher, adding to the winter air. Kristina is in trouble for hurting the feelings of another student.

Mr. Wesley has been a hard one to figure. His outward demeanor is kind and quiet. His spirit has been harder to discern. We made a great effort to have him understand Asperger's, and how it relates to his student, Kristina. We have tried to encourage him, and let him know that Kristina's corrections are not to be taken personally. He seems to try to understand, but we are not convinced that he does understand. It has made it a difficult year for us. Ironically, Mr. Wesley is Kristina's favorite teacher to date.

Nevertheless, another situation regarding Kristina's behavior needed our attention. We spoke to Kristina, and she swore she did not say what the teacher or student said she said. However, the words repeated to us by Mr. Wesley echo the word choices of our daughter. Something wasn't right. Finally, it clicked.

"Kristina, did you tell Chloe that she is annoying?"

"No."

"Do you think she is annoying?"

"Yes. She is such a tattle tale."

"Kristina, let's try something. I want you to repeat after me. Say 'I like blue!'"

"I LIKE BLUE!"

"Now, let's try it a little quieter. 'I like blue.' "

"I like blue."

"Now whisper it."

"I like blue," whispered Kristina.

"Now, think it, but don't say it."

I looked at Kristina. She pressed her lips together, and sounded out a muted "I like blue" through pursed lips. We tried a few more times. Every time, Kristina could not "think it, not say it."

We had a breakthrough.

It all made sense. In a way, they were all right. In her mind, Kristina did not tell Chloe that she thought she was annoying. In reality, Kristina said it quietly, not to Chloe, but to herself. Therefore, Kristina was guilty of saying it, and a child's feelings were hurt.

That stunk.

But I was ecstatic.

I had found another key I needed to share with the school. But would Mr. Wesley believe me?

Chapter Three

The 504 Plan

I don't need to learn anything because I know everything already.

— Kristina's written response to the 1st grade topic, "What do you hope to learn in school this year?"

Quite frankly, the diagnostic process, coupled with the initial dealings with the school, can be time consuming, not to mention emotionally overwhelming. After all, work schedules need readjusting to accommodate meetings and tests. The child has her schedule disrupted, too, not to mention a good deal of interaction with strangers. Paperwork via forms and questionnaires come from all angles, needing to be copied for personal files before being sent back out. Somewhere, in the middle of all this, insurance steps into the picture, even if only briefly. There is a lot to do, and a lot to learn.

Knowing that your family is under a microscope is uncomfortable, regardless of the motive. Even if the events proceed smoothly, stress can still rear its head. Stress, good or bad, is still stress. During this time, we found it important to learn when to say "no" to extra activities and commitments. On the flip side, it was important to keep up whatever activity gave us strength, be it church, a hobby, or simple walks. One phrase from Kristina's baby days forever rings in my head: If you don't take care of yourself, you can't adequately take care of your family. Of course, this didn't mean dropping all chores, and forever choosing takeout, but it meant carving out some emotional downtime on a regular basis. Still, it can be hard.

All in all, we have been told we are fortunate that Kristina was diagnosed with Asperger's early. But having an early diagnosis doesn't make the road smoother; we just happened to get on it a few exits earlier than many other folks. Our hope was to take advantage of this early diagnosis, learning the bends and potholes before reaching middle school.

Even with the diagnosis, it would be over two years before a formal education plan would emerge. The process itself, once started, took a long time to complete. If I could sum up our response to the special services process in a few words, it would be: perseverance, focus, kindness, self-education, perseverance, discernment, patience, perseverance, faith.

Did I mention perseverance?

Or the willingness to move on, if a hill or two aren't worth dying for?

Immediately after Kristina's testing began, the school was quick to supply her with the service we all thought she needed the most: social skills training. She began to meet with the caseworker for weekly social skills training. We asked if we needed to sit down with the school to form some kind of formalized plan before it went underway, but school assured us it wasn't necessary. Kristina now had a diagnosis, and, as a result, the school was willing to provide this type of training for her. That seemed okay with us, since they decided to provide this service without all the red tape. At the time, we were grateful. Hey, who doesn't mind skipping the red tape? After all, we knew nothing about formal education plans, or their place in the educational food chain.

However, just as Aspie's are not naturally socially intuitive, parents are not naturally intuitive when it comes to special education, plans, and services. We discovered the hard way that it would have been better to push for a formalized plan from the beginning. Since she did not receive a formal plan until the end of third grade, a full review before middle school was less likely. That is not a good thing. There is no way we could have known this would be the case. Just like our kids need to be taught social skills and nuances, we, likewise, need to be taught the Special Education process.

As a former teacher of mine once said, we don't learn via osmosis.

However, there are days it seems that it sure would be easier to sit on some sort of thick, special education processes, plans, and procedures book for an hour or two than learning all the lingo, laws, and loopholes.

The sea of special education is vast and full. There are terms, laws, and all sorts of things to make a parent's head swim, not to mention the fact that many of the rules and services vary from state to state—even district to district. We did the best we could at the time. We read. We questioned. We listened. Although we picked up some pink pearls along the way, our knowledge remained limited.

Looking back, I'm not sure what we would have done differently. We asked around, trying to understand the process the best we could. All we knew was that Kristina really needed some assistance with social skills, so were quite happy she was going to receive some help. After all, we wanted what was best for her. At the time this seemed to fit the bill. Regardless, during first grade, Kristina began her entry into the world of special services. She began to meet weekly with the caseworker.

Kristina continued working with the caseworker for the remainder of first grade, and all through second. Although initially relieved she was getting needed attention, we quickly became disenchanted. Our small number of conversations with the woman showed she truly attempted to understand Asperger's, but her lack of communication with us left us largely in the dark as to Kristina's progress. Our feedback from the caseworker was typically a result of our persistence to acquire it. We wanted so badly to understand what Kristina was working on, which tools she was using, even what we could do to back up her training at home. However, much was promised, and little delivered. It was a very disappointing experience.

Our attempts at getting to know the caseworker personally did not go very far, either. We felt as if we were continually suspect, her intention to judge us, not work with us. The odd thing was, face to face conversations seemed to go fine, though phone conversations—her primary mode of communication—were emotionally draining and difficult for me. As a result of our interpretation of her body language and communication style, we may very well have misjudged her.

Meanwhile, Kristina's time spent with social skills training did not seem to be paying off in the classroom. Calls from both the first and second grade teachers (both wonderful teachers) came in, with a concern here or there about Kristina's classroom behavior.

Those calls are always a joy.

Just like finding a rip in your stocking after arriving at work.

During a snowstorm.

During all of this, Kristina informed us how many days Mrs. Second Grade had worn clothes with buttons.

Apparently, the button aversion was still alive and well.

In the beginning of third grade, we met with Kristina's teacher, and solicited his thoughts on continuing social skills training. No other services were suggested by the school, especially as Kristina's academics were stellar. Her teacher commented that he would like to see how the year flowed before putting her back with the caseworker. He wanted to see what he could manage himself, and appeared quite optimistic he could work successfully with Kristina in the classroom.

Quite frankly, we were a bit relieved. Kristina had a year off of what seemed to be a weekly commitment with little or no results.

As third grade progressed, it became evident that no matter how much her teacher tried to understand Kristina and where she was coming from, he had few successes. No matter how much we tried to help him understand, he gave the impression of struggling to comprehend it all. It was frustrating on all sides.

On a cold, harsh, winter's day, we received a note from her teacher, saying there was much difficulty with Kristina in class, and we needed to meet. At the meeting, he suggested Kristina go before the Pupil Assistance Team (PAT). This was the first step towards a working document that would assure Kristina had what is required by law as a Free Appropriate Public Education (FAPE). There was a good chance Kristina would wind up with either an Individualized Education Plan (IEP) or 504 plan. In other words, we were on our way towards a formal educational plan for Kristina. We agreed with the teacher that the PAT meeting was a good idea.

A full two years after the diagnosis, thus began our introduction to "EAS" (Educational Alphabet Soup).

Shortly afterwards, I received an unexpected phone call from the caseworker. She, not the teacher, would be our contact for this process.

Her tone was characteristically businesslike as she interrogated me, while telling me about the upcoming PAT meeting. Instead of focusing mostly on Kristina, the call seemed to hone in on our home life. Not only did the call throw me off guard, it left me perplexed, and feeling as if my home had been stormed. During the call, I found myself bracing against the door, letting out only information pertinent to my daughter's success in school. I stood my ground, visualizing my daughter, what's best for her, and our family. Still, it felt like she was coming at me with a crowbar, trying to pry all sorts of information out of me, most of which had nothing to do with Kristina, school, or Asperger's. Our family has nothing to hide. We can't even dance. Nevertheless, we are private people, not wanting to bare our souls to an unknown world, either. I may have misread her intent, but the experience was quite unpleasant, leaving me confused and rattled.

Like many parents of a child with Asperger's, I felt as if she, (or the school through her), firmly suspected us as either the root of Kristina's struggles, or a grand part of it, not neurological wiring. I felt as if she was doing her dead level best to find something, anything, to pin on us, instead of considering Kristina's biological makeup.

Even though thoroughly investigating the family's personal life is most likely a typical procedure, this experience was not only unpleasant, but bordered on the arrogant. There was no sense of trust in our family, nor an air of willingness to understand it. For example, she once commented how Kristina repeatedly refused to look at her to acknowledge her. A simple scholar should know one marker of Asperger's is lack of eye contact. Merely telling my daughter to look at someone in the eyes during conversation will not automatically, and definitively, change that behavior. Somehow, the caseworker never seemed to make those connections.

Years later, I still do not comprehend the intended purpose behind that call. It still leaves a sting.

The conversation ended with promised notification of the time and date of the PAT meeting. As this particular meeting is solely amongst school personnel, notification was more to let us know the ball was rolling, than anything else.

Days and weeks passed by, and we heard nothing, which was not surprising considering her previous lack of follow through with communication. As there was no way of knowing if the meeting had yet been held, or even scheduled, I initiated contact and, finally, somehow, got the promised information.

At last, the meeting was scheduled. The first concrete step to formalizing recognition of Kristina's struggles in an academic setting was underway. Simply put, it was all going down in writing. Kristina was finally going to have a formal plan.

As meetings and phone calls ramped up for Kristina's plan, we continually had to stop whichever educator we were communicating with to have them explain all the lingo, as well as the process.

At every step.

It may seem tedious and tiresome for these individuals to do this for every family, but it is very necessary. My husband and I are the types who will ask whenever we don't understand something, but not everyone is that way. In fact, some people, not wanting to appear ignorant, will act as if they do understand, being largely lost all the while. How can that be good for the child?

There also can be the sense that the school is handling everything appropriately, and in a timely fashion, so sit back, relax, and wait to hear from them. It's the "don't call us, we'll call you" phenomenon. Unfortunately, "assuming" is not wise. It is imperative for the guardians to be active in understanding the process, as well as advocating, tirelessly, for their child. We wouldn't build a house without periodically checking in on the site.

How much more important is the educational and developmental foundation of our child?

We tried to be rational and realistic when it came to goals for our daughter, as well as the length of time it took to complete the process. We tried not to micromanage the situation. We tried to keep in mind that the school's best interest is in the child's *education*, not every other aspect under the sun.

Though there were days I wish they could gives us tools for expanding her food preferences.

Or keeping her room neat.

We debated pushing for consideration of an IEP (Individualized Education Plan) over a 504 plan. Both plans are nationally recognized, which is good if relocating. However, although the 504 plan is upheld by the school, it was explained to us that it is not considered as strong or as thorough as the IEP, nor does it require as frequent formal updating. The 504 is also done "in-house," while the IEP goes before the Committee on Special Education (CSE).

In general, both plans state the student's disability as it relates to school and learning. Both plans list specific modifications and suggestions for educators to take into consideration. The plans mention any need for special services, such as social skills training, and occupational therapy (OT). They also mention any need for specific classroom modifications, such as a separate place for testing. Every educator who works with the student during that specific year reviews and signs the plan. Parents do meet with those involved in the planning process, give input, also signing off on it. Creating a plan is truly a team effort. (More information on both the 504 plan and the IEP is available at local schools and numerous websites, which can provide much more detailed and appropriate information than provided here. What I have written is our personal experience and understanding at the time.)

After the PAT met, our contact promised us that Kristina would receive a 504 plan. We asked about why the 504 vs. an IEP, and were told that they felt an IEP was not appropriate for Kristina at this point. We did not know what to do. We decided to check around, and solicit opinions from the few parents we knew who had been through this type of process.

After talking to several people familiar with both plans, we discovered the following (which is to be assumed as personal opinion, only). If we are given what we feel Kristina needs in a 504 plan, and the school can be trusted to uphold it, then have peace, and be done with it. Another reason given was for the sake of our child and our family. From what we could ascertain, the IEP process is not only long and bureaucratic, but can be an emotional drain on the family. We heard several emotional stories of how the IEP meeting seemed like a cold dissection of the child and family. Being new to the process, the thought of going through the wringer, yet again, was less than appealing. We had already had a taste of that, and desired no more. All we wanted was for Kristina's diagnosis to be recognized by the school, and for her to receive the basic help needed to function successfully in an academic setting. We didn't think it was too much to ask, nor warranting a full committee's analysis and approval.

In short, the IEP process seemed daunting. The 504 process seemed more personable, and equally helpful.

The school had indeed proven itself not only trustworthy, but also generally acted in the best interest of our daughter. They sincerely tried. Again, having no experience with either plan, we went with our gut, and with what made the most sense at the time. We settled for the 504 plan.

Looking back, would an IEP have been better? Not in the short run. Kristina received all promised services, as well as any special considerations suggested. In fact, the school referred Kristina to OT, and immediately began those services after receiving the prescription from her pediatrician. One pothole we discovered in fourth grade would have occurred 504, IEP, ABCDEFG, or not. However, satisfaction over the long run is another story. With middle school approaching, it would have been preferable to have a plan that required the school to review it yearly.

No matter how many questions we asked early on, we didn't know. No one provided that information to us, and we didn't think to ask about the review process. We weren't yet fluent in Educational Alphabet Soup.

Come to think of it, we still aren't.

At least we have reached the intermediate level.

Finally, all school personnel interacting with Kristina would know that she has Asperger's, and about any struggles accompanying it. This was key. We were surprised to learn that, up to this point, (two years after her diagnosis) the special teachers, such as the music teacher, never knew of her diagnosis. It was briefly explained to us that, because of all the privacy laws, the school could not inform any personnel, excluding her homeroom teacher and specialists, of Kristina's diagnosis without the proper paperwork. (Again, this was our personal experience, not to be considered universal.) We were glad to know that, from that point on, everyone who worked with Kristina would know she has Asperger's, and how it manifests itself in her. In short, it was validity that Kristina had something needing attention and modification.

It wasn't just a difficult personality.

It wasn't her home life.

It wasn't ADD.

It was Asperger's Syndrome, plain and simple.

Truth be told, experiencing the school process is much like being thrown into another culture, with no guidebook or translator. We had abbreviations and numbers thrown at us with no explanation unless we asked. IEP, OT, 504, PT, etc. I cannot stress enough the need for the school to provide some sort of plain and simple handbook or flyer for the parents as their child enters the arena of special services. A flow chart would work wonders, too. Parents should not have to press for understanding of basic terminology, or ask for a roadmap—not only of the current process, but for future ones, as well.

After we decided on the 504 plan, we asked the caseworker, and her teacher, how long it would be before we would have the rough plan to look at. Kristina's teacher admitted it was a long, slow process. However, he told us we would have a general idea in about a month. That seemed fair. He also told us the caseworker was our contact for this process. That was around March.

March came and went.

April came and went.

Likewise May. I ran into Kristina's teacher in the hallway, and expressed to him my disappointment and confusion as to the lack of communication from the school. He sounded surprised that we had not heard back from the caseworker. He asked me if I had spoken with the principal. I told him no, and he thanked me, expressing his gratitude for not getting his friends in trouble. I thanked him for his time.

And went home dumbfounded.

Thank you for not getting my friends in trouble by not getting the principal involved? What? Whatever happened to the mindset that educators have only the best interests of the kids at heart? Did I hear him right? Was I just thanked for putting the protection of the educators over timely and promised help for my child? I could feel wrinkles furrowing deeper into my brow. Very rarely am I speechless. This was one of those times.

One teacher, whom I befriended, would routinely ask how things were going. When I confided in her that we had waited months for that which was promised to take weeks, she gave me golden advice I took and used. She confided in me that, in her experience, the parents who press for information and dates are the families who got results. It was the squeaky wheel phenomenon. I went home that day, mulled over the unanswered e-mails and empty promises of the past several months, the very recent conversation with Kristina's teacher, and acted on her advice.

I squeaked.

I sent an e-mail to the principal.

It worked.

I heard back immediately from the principal. The following day, I heard from the school's psychologist (not the caseworker, nor the psychologist we met with in first grade), informing me that they had scheduled a time for us to go over Kristina's 504 plan with her and her teacher—within the week. On top of this, she was our new contact for the plan.

Coincidence?

I sometimes wonder what would have happened if I had never contacted the principal. It was already June, so I doubt we would have heard anything before late August. I confided my suspicions in my friend, and she agreed. We both shook our heads as we thought of other families who do not understand how much they need to pursue the school on these matters. Thanks be to God she informed me about the unspoken process.

We genuinely looked forward to the 504 plan meeting. It was a huge step toward recognition, on behalf of the school, that Kristina was more than bright and perpetually stubborn. It was also our chance, as her parents, to show the school that we were grounded and supportive of our daughter, as well as the school's efforts. We wanted to show the school that we wanted to work with them, not fight them. We wanted to show the school we were trying to be open-minded, while at the same time doing what we believe to be best for our daughter.

The morning of the 504 plan was warm and sunny. Still, my husband and I felt like we were walking through fog. We signed in at the main office, and made the short walk down to the school psychologist's office.

The office was small and bright. A young woman, with short dark hair, sat at a small table, greeting us with a warm smile. Her youth made my husband and I wince inside, as we wondered how much experience she could really have with a kid like Kristina. We sat down, introducing ourselves.

As we waited in the small office for Kristina's teacher, we exchanged chitchat. Finally, we watched as Kristina's class passed by on the way to the music room. A few moments later, Kristina's teacher popped his head in, with his characteristic dimpled smile, to say hello. As he did, his face whitened as he realized he had completely forgotten about our meeting.

My husband and I couldn't believe it. This meeting had been months in the making. We were under the impression that any meeting about a 504 plan was a very important meeting, especially the first one.

And her teacher had forgotten all about it.

As the meeting unfolded, it became evident that the psychologist was not very familiar with Kristina. She remarked that her comments were largely based on information provided to her by the school, not so much knowledge of Kristina, herself. At one point, she suggested the possibility that Kristina might have been misdiagnosed, and that we should honestly consider having her re-diagnosed with more soup: NVLD (Nonverbal Learning Disorder).

My husband and I were flabbergasted.

Okay, a young, relatively inexperienced person, who had barely interacted with our child, is suggesting changing a diagnosis made by several professionals with years of experience with kids like Kristina? Including one, in particular, who has known our daughter since birth?

Sure, why not? Where do we sign the papers?

Thankfully, Kristina's teacher wasn't convinced.

As the psychologist pointed out markers of NVLD, Kristina's teacher consistently disagreed that they applied to Kristina. His remarks gave us breath. (In fact, he suggested that she advise future teachers to read up on and become familiar with Asperger's Syndrome.)

Andrew and I did our best to speak calmly as we refuted the psychologist's suggestion. We did not understand the impetus behind such a strong suggestion, especially when refuted by her teacher, the person in the school who should know Kristina best.

Then it dawned on us. We asked her if she had experience with any girls who had Asperger's. She thought for a moment, then shook her head as she replied "No." All the cases she was familiar with concerned boys. Her tone appeared to change after that.

Kristina would be much better off if the school did not compare her solely to boys with Asperger's. Just as there are differences between neurologically "normal" girls and boys, there are differences between girls and boys with Asperger's. According to an article by Tony Attwood, *The Pattern of Ability and Development of Girls with Asperger's Syndrome,* September 1999, he mentions that special interests of boys tend to revolve around such topics as transportation, while girls lean toward animals and classic literature. In the case of boys, intense interest in transportation may facilitate a diagnosis of Asperger's, while a girl's interest in animals is likely to be "dismissed as simply typical of young girls."

Also, according to Dr. Attwood, peer groups influence these children. Girls, for instance, tend to be more inclusive and "mothering," while boys tend to be more exclusive and "predatory" to the point of bullying. This difference between boys and girls with Asperger's is not insignificant.

To a casual observer, it may appear that the girl and boy are quite different, and, therefore, unlikely to share the same diagnosis. Unfortunately, such an assumption only promises greater misunderstanding of the girl, resulting in a host of additional difficulties.

Consider the playground at recess. Imagine two children with Asperger's Syndrome; one a boy, the other a girl. The boy is teased by his peers. Some may even mock his way of speaking, or his special interest, and, unfortunately, physically bully him. The boy is typically left to play on his own. The girl, on the other hand, is seen interacting with other girls. When the girl makes an inappropriate reaction, another girl comes along side to correct her, or to redirect her. In addition, as Dr. Attwood phrases it, "They may prompt the child when they are unsure of what to do or say in social situations. …" Observation alone makes it easy to assume that the girl is "fitting in." But closer observation will show that her peers mitigate her social awkwardness, which is not generally what boys do. Still, the social awkwardness of the girl excludes her from full inclusion with her peers.

Dr. Attwood's article is a great source for anyone interested in reading more about the differences between boys and girls diagnosed with Asperger's Syndrome.

Later on, I mentioned the 504 review meeting to Kristina's pediatrician. Her reaction was nearly identical to mine. She appeared quite upset that the school would suggest Kristina's diagnosis was incorrect. She even provided copies of paperwork from Kristina's diagnosis to present to the school, even highlighting key points and facts in support of it. The diagnosis from Developmental Services Center, and Kristina's pediatrician, stands.

Kristina is Kristina is Krissy.

End of story.

Sort of.

Fast forward to the fall of fifth grade...

Another school psychologist, in the same elementary school, again barely familiar with Kristina, suggested a change in her diagnosis, stating the possibility that her Asperger's diagnosis is incorrect. Again, we were floored. As last time, I asked her about her experience working with Aspies. She mentioned she had much experience, telling how she was currently working with a group of children who had Asperger's. I asked her specifically about her experience working with *girls* with Asperger's. She paused, stating that the group was composed solely of boys, and that she really couldn't think of any girls she had ever worked with who had Asperger's.

Bingo.

Here we go again. Time to repeat the subject of boys vs. girls.

One of my daughter's favorite subjects.

I find it ironic that the very people who see life on a grayscale fail to see the gradations from Aspie to Aspie. In other words, just because this Aspie doesn't act the same as the others you have met, doesn't mean she does not have Asperger's.

It doesn't mean the doctors who diagnosed her are wrong.

It doesn't mean her parents have some obsession about having a child diagnosed with autism.

It simply means that Asperger's is different from person to person, just as hair color, height, or any other thing that makes us all human.

In the meantime, Kristina regularly met with a therapist who has extensive experience with autism spectrum disorders, and who even trained staff at the Developmental Services Center. I trusted her opinion, and knew she would shoot straight. I spoke with her about the resurfacing suggestion of altering Kristina's Asperger diagnosis. She, like Kristina's pediatrician, concurred with the diagnosis of Asperger's. She assured us that she could also provide the school with another diagnosis of Asperger's Syndrome, atop of the one provided by the Center, if it came to that. She even agreed to speak with the school on behalf of Kristina. We took her up on her offer, and solicited her help.

Rewinding back to the end of third grade…

Back at the meeting, Kristina's teacher confessed to us that it took well over half the year for him to realize that Kristina was not trying to make life difficult for him. Perhaps that was his way of communicating encouragement regarding Kristina's behaviors, a sort of backhanded compliment? In all fairness, one thing we have continually desired from Kristina's educators is frankness. Still, that frankness can hurt.

Another time, an educator described Kristina as an animated, funny, energetic character written about in children's books.

But one you'd rather read about, than have bounding all over your classroom.

How do you respond to that? It was a forthright opinion, and the intention wasn't to make us feel bad, but rather to paint a picture of Kristina in the classroom setting. But it stung. And still stings—even as I type. But we'd rather have that frankness than insincere politeness, or silence.

Early on, we tried to convince her teacher not to take Kristina's actions personally, as he had for several months. We chose specific examples, such as Kristina correcting simple mistakes that teachers seldom make, like grammatical errors on the blackboard. We told him that when Kristina does that it's because, in her mind, she sees something that needs fixing. And, if anything, she views her comments as helpful, not disrespectful. In fact, often times, Kristina finds it offensive to leave mistakes uncorrected. Sorry to say, our comments took many months to sink in. Her teacher had to discover Kristina's motives all on his own. Meanwhile, Kristina went over half of third grade reaping repercussions from being misunderstood, often being overlooked for tasks and other encouragements, as her actions were interpreted as disrespect. Thankfully, Kristina did not pick up on much of it.

As the 504 plan review meeting wrapped up, we thanked the psychologist for her time. We finally had a rough document in hand. It was good.

As we walked up the hallway back toward the main office, our emotions were a mix of relief and confusion. The final outcome was all we could ask for. The process itself was draining. Andrew hurried back to work, while I went straight home. Once inside, I sat down and journaled the entire experience.

Third grade came to a close, and the final 504 plan looked like a good fit. Things with school were not perfect, but they sure seemed to try. As much as we felt her third grade teacher took a while understanding our child and Asperger's, he did give us nuggets, which helped for fourth grade. Earlier in the year, he pointed out that the girls, who up to this point had been generally tolerant and inclusive, would start to "clique up" in the spring. His words rang true, and our concerns, which until then largely focused on our daughter's education and appropriate classroom behaviors, now begun to spread to her peers. We had already noticed that the (birthday) party train of her younger years was coming to a screeching halt. Stories of sleepovers were newsreels for Kristina, not experiences. The pain named "exclusion" was beginning to awaken.

The end-of-the-year family party, closing out third grade, was rough. Kristina beamed, trying to get her teacher's attention at various points during lunch, receiving a mere "hello" along the way. Kristina was not the only one experiencing exclusion, though. Other students who were higher maintenance than most, seemed to share the same experience. It was heart wrenching watching those few kids—and the look on their parent's faces, as they struggled to gain more than a morsel of their teacher's attention. From a mother's perspective, it appeared that Kristina's teacher's focus was on the easier kids, not all the kids.

No matter how much we had tried to support and encourage the teacher over the past year, the final moments of school proved we had not been entirely effective. I wish I knew what we could have done differently. The thought of that day still pinches my heart.

Thank goodness, Kristina was oblivious, still unable to read this type of social cue, or her heart would have been crushed that day. This was one of her favorite teachers.

At least this teacher made Kristina laugh and smile.

PINK PEARLS

for Chapter Three

FOR THE CAREGIVERS

. . . .

Take care of yourself!

The best way to fully be there for your child is to take care of yourself. Keep (or add) what gives you strength. Delete what doesn't.

Get out of the soup!

Go beyond asking what the acronyms *stand for*. Ask what they *mean*.

Journal it!

Write down each interaction with the school, including the dates, in a specific notebook or binder. If crunched for time, one or two sentences work fine.

Visualize your child

When the world is shaking, and the walls are tumbling in, picture your child in your mind's eye.

Asperger's in Pink

Consider asking the school if they have experience with *girls* and Asperger's

Be proactive in the process

Make sure to follow up with the school, at reasonable intervals, with reasonable expectations. Keep your tone of voice in check, no matter how high your anxieties or frustrations may be. Try to be as objective as possible. Have a desire to work with the school, and let them know you do indeed wish to work *together*.

Know who to "go-to"

Understand who your school contact is, and the best way to communicate with each other.

Never assume

Do not assume that all school personnel are aware of your child's diagnosis. Understand how the privacy laws work in your district, and how such information is (or is not) made accessible to whom.

Boil it all down

Do not overwhelm the school with demands. Carefully examine your requests, making them as reasonable as possible.

FOR THE EDUCATORS

· ·

Patience makes perfect

Be prepared—mentally and practically speaking—to carefully define special education terms and processes to every caregiver. Approach each new case with the intention of helping them understand the process before moving on to the planning phase.

Make it easy

By making it simple for families to understand and navigate the system, you help create a more peaceable environment for everyone involved.

Map it!

Consider creating a simple map or flow-chart of the special education process (including review schedules) for the caregivers. It should begin with the child's current grade, carrying her to the end of high school. Flow charts are best, as it is often impossible to know what plans and services she will need even a few years away. It will also help those families already familiar with special education, but new to the district.

View each child individually

Resist the urge to compare the new Aspie to others, especially if experience with girls (or even boys) on the spectrum is limited.

Meet the parents with an open mind

Resist the habit of classifying parents in light of the child's behavior. It may well be that the problems are genuinely neuro-biological in nature, and that the parents need optimistic support and encouragement just as much as the student.

FOR EVERYONE

Communication is key

Determine the most effective means of communication, and apply it. Is it creating a visual map of the process? Is it something simple, like a daily sticker system? Make sure that goals and expectations are clear, and tools accessible.

New school district + old plan = regrouping

Make sure to meet early on, before the child enters school, as the processes, services, and expectations can vary from district to district.

WHAT I WISH WE HAD AVAILABLE

A flow-chart of the process, and a simple glossary of terms handed to us by the school

INSIDE the
BUBBLE

But I Want to Know!

The time slowly ticked down from the red and black sign overhead. The darkness of the train station lent an eerie air. Only a few minutes left until the train that would take us back to the parking lot arrived. Thankfully, a metal bench in the middle of the platform provided seating after what had been a long, but enjoyable day. Kristina's class had been studying the formation of our country, with Philadelphia playing a major role in her lessons.

Like most kids, Kristina protested going to historical sites for vacation. After all, there were no rides, no games, and certainly no princesses here. But the light in her eyes as she heard the park rangers speak of history, which occurred in the very places where we stood, showed an appreciation for the trip. We walked all over the historical part of the city, and Kristina had held up rather well.

Going into Independence Hall, we had to pass our belongings, including jackets, through a scanning device, much like one at the airport. The heightened security was new to us, but only a small inconvenience.

To Kristina, it made no sense.

"Why do I have to take my jacket off?" Kristina questioned.

"Everyone has to place their jackets through the machine. The people who work here need to make sure no one is bringing anything dangerous into the building," I answered.

"I have nothing in my jacket. I don't want to take it off. This is stupid," she protested.

"Kristina," I continued, "you don't have a choice. We all have to do this."

"But I don't want to take my jacket off. I don't have anything in it," exclaimed Kristina at normal volume.

Andrew and I did all we could to remain calm. I became anxious that Kristina's reluctance to conform would prevent us from going through. Finally, Kristina placed her jacket on the belt. We were through, but not without some disapproving looks.

Now we sat and waited for the train out of the city. Thankfully, Kristina remained on the bench. Her lack of spatial awareness makes me a nervous wreck anytime we wait for an underground train. A friend of mine once told me of tending to people who fell onto such tracks. Recalling that conversation, a shiver ran down my spine.

Out of the corner of my eye, I could see a man acting suspiciously, and so did Andrew. His mannerisms, among other things, left me feeling quite uncomfortable. I glanced back at the timer. One minute and twenty seconds left to go. We shot each other a knowing glance, hoping he would leave, or at least walk away from our stop. During our silent communication, Kristina's voice rang out, loud and clear.

"Did you see that man do that? Why did he do that?"

A twinge of fear raced through me. Did he hear her? If he did, what would happen?

"Kristina," I whispered, "please do not comment about anyone right now."

"Why?" replied Kristina, with her usual tone.

"Just trust me Kristina, okay?"

"But I want to know...," continued Kristina, at full volume.

The train arrived before Kristina could finish, and we made our way into the car, thankful to leave our suspicions, and the stranger, back on the platform.

Just when you think you have gone over every scenario imaginable for the afternoon, life takes another turn.

Chapter Four

Occupational Therapy and "Group"

KRISTINA ON ETIQUETTE: *"What's the point of manners?"*

The last day of third grade ended with a bang. Kristina marched up our long, black driveway with a sour look on her face. Of all the choices for fourth grade teachers, Kristina was assigned to the one we dreaded. Kristina lamented the fact she did not get the teacher she wanted, though the most popular girl did. All we could hope for was that her years of teaching might prove helpful in understanding our daughter.

That hope was dashed.

Fourth grade proved a bear regarding Kristina's regular classroom experience. Looking back over my journal I ran across an entry, which pretty much summed up any random day during the fourth grade:

> *Fourth Grade: Life isn't what you picture it. And today, I feel that the pieces have been dumped upside down, the box lid still missing. At least the sun decided to shine.*

Truthfully, none of the fourth grade teachers seemed an ideal fit for Kristina. Unfortunately, this teacher's brand of strictness, along with humor drenched with sarcasm, negatively affected her all year, her tone becoming increasingly stern and unforgiving. Her natural joy and bounce eroded, to the point of anger on our part. On top of that, her teacher acted like someone with little or no desire to adhere fully to any 504 plan.

Early on, we could sense that something was not right with Kristina and school. For the first few months, we wondered if Kristina was simply full of hormones, or manifesting her difficulty transitioning to a new grade in a cantankerous way. She became increasingly moody and combative. We wondered if her teacher had anything to do with it, but tried to chalk it up to a growing girl. But the second half of Christmas break, we got our daughter back. It took halfway into that week for her true self to reemerge. Her sense of humor returned, as did her level of patience. My husband and I were the same Andrew and Julie. The house was the same charming home. Work and church hadn't changed. Everything was the same.

Except school.

Kristina's behaviors during fourth grade were disconcerting. One thing our daughter does is mimic the mannerisms of her teachers. Just as her play revolved around shopping and doctor visits during her earliest years, it now evolved to include school. It's been an interesting view into her world. One teacher seemed humorous, another like a fair drill sergeant, yet another kind and soft-spoken. Her interpretation of her fourth grade teacher reflected someone not only funny, but also someone who yelled—a lot.

Stories Kristina would tell at home were a mix of grand humor, great teaching, and a horrible lack of patience. We had heard rumors about this particular teacher. Some were large and seemingly unbelievable. Unfortunately, some proved true.

Communication from her teacher rivaled that of the caseworker, keeping in contact with us next to never. We often, though not incessantly, asked the teacher for insight into her classroom struggles. We simply wanted her "take" on the situation. We went to her first, before bringing our concerns to the principal. We tried to be objective, but it was difficult.

Almost every correspondence was ignored.

One thing my husband and I have always said is that the school cannot expect us to support what they are doing if they do not adequately communicate with us. If there are classroom concerns with Kristina, we need to know so we can work with her at home. My assumption is that a nine year old is not going to volunteer any incriminating information.

Unless it is about another nine year old.

Her lack of communication, coupled with upsetting stories Kristina brought home, had us quite concerned. We wanted ever so much to discern truth from misunderstanding. Was Kristina overblowing it? Was she misinterpreting her sarcasm as biting truth? Were some comments merely her version of humor, simply misunderstood by Kristina? Were her stern remarks to mischievous students merely firmness, or were they indeed sprinkled with malicious intent? If there was more to these stories than Kristina told, we needed to speak with our daughter, and explain the situation. We needed to talk with the teacher, letting her know that Kristina was taking her all too seriously.

But if she was right, we wanted the principal involved.

We suspect that our persistence annoyed this particular teacher. However, our concerns lay with helping our daughter, not making the teacher's life easier, especially when Kristina's life seemed to be increasingly difficult and confusing at school. Those with Asperger's learn by what they see around them, not unlike most people. During the week, she saw more of her teacher than she saw of us. For a child who learns by observation, it became increasingly apparent she was seeing quite a bit of "do as I say, not as I do." According to Kristina, this teacher had a knack for breaking her own classroom rules.

This situation had to be addressed.

But how?

Over halfway through the year, her frustration with Kristina and another student came to a head. Kristina has consistently struggled with group work. Her 504 plan specifically identifies her struggles with teamwork. This was something for her teacher to expect. However, she and another student were not working well together, so the teacher split them up. It was during Social Studies, during a project. From all we could ascertain, both kids were at fault for not getting along. She had the one child join another group. Even though she knew Kristina struggles in this area, she had Kristina sit alone at her desk, causing her to miss out on the project. We found out about this incident from Kristina. Had she not told us, we would have assumed all was well.

After months of being left in the dark regardless of our efforts, we called a meeting with the principal. We began by bringing up the Social Studies incident. The principal remained quiet, taking in the dialogue. It was an uncomfortable meeting, but vital, nonetheless.

The meeting was partially successful. The teacher agreed to restart weekly communication, but that lasted only a few weeks. On a more important note, she admitted her actions regarding the Social Studies project. Kristina was right.

She apologized.

This event gave us a slight taste of the discrimination kids with special needs unfortunately experience. This taste, bitter and acidic, still lingers.

In spite of all this, we remained optimistic. We hoped the next teacher would be a better fit. With twinges of sadness and frustration, we figured we would spend much of the summer undoing the erosion of Kristina's behavior patterns and tone of voice—not to mention her emotions.

It's funny; it seems as if many people feel that a child's behavior is *mostly* a reflection of the home. I'm sure that is true in some part. However, when your child spends most of her functioning hours at school, her behavior *will* reflect school.

Asperger's in Pink

I think one reason for her difficulties with this teaching style lies in the way external information is processed. For example, most kids pick up on sarcasm, and interpret it as such. However, sometimes Kristina gets sarcasm, and other times she doesn't. Kristina sees the world as literal, largely black and white. In addition, many kids would interpret the teacher's stern behavior as a signal to sit still and behave. Kristina takes it as a reason to fear, as well as an injustice. To Kristina, (perceived) negative behavior is something to be revealed and confronted, not something to tolerate. It is something hypocritical, and that something does not compute. It is something to shout from the mountaintops as appalling, wrong, and needing to be changed.

Hers is the kind of attitude to applaud.

Hers is the attitude that makes leaders, not followers.

It's also the kind of attitude, with the accompanying action, that gives parents gray hair.

Or makes them go bald.

More than once we had to remind Kristina not to talk back to her teacher, or correct her, no matter how far she thought she bent the rules. We did direct her to speak with "trusted" personnel in the school, if she felt things were getting to be a bit much. Doing so also allowed others at school to help her put Mrs. Fourth Grade's actions into perspective.

Sometimes, Kristina overreacted and her actions did *not* reflect what she painted. Many times, she simply misread her teacher.

Unfortunately, Kristina's dislike of her teacher was evident, furthering the chasm between her and her classmates. They lauded Mrs. Fourth Grade, while Kristina prayed for home schooling.

On top of it all, the lack of regular communication, resulting in a lack of relationship with this teacher, left us in the same position as with the caseworker. We may have very well misjudged the individual. But will we ever know? One thing we do know, our daughter had one miserable year of school.

We encouraged Kristina to confide in the school psychologist, as well as her personal therapist. We knew that school was rough, and she did not feel comfortable with her teacher. She did share that she told the psychologist things from time to time, but that the psychologist never said much. Truth be told, we don't know if she acted on any of Kristina's information, but at least she heard concerns from Kristina herself, not just her parents.

Thankfully, fourth grade did not consist solely of the homeroom. Thankfully, Kristina continued OT.

Occupational therapy was the sunshine of fourth grade. OT was a godsend. Before Kristina started OT, her sensory world was in grand disarray. Assemblies and videos continued to be problematic for her. Her tactile defensiveness was also in high gear. It seemed as if Kristina could not sense rough sensations, but bristled at light ones, as if they were dangerous. It was not uncommon (and still is not) for Kristina to acquire a bruise or significant scrape, having no idea where it came from.

Sometimes, her inability to recognize certain bumps and bruises resulted in delayed medical attention. In third grade, Kristina came home with a goose egg on her head from bumping it pretty hard on the playground equipment. The lunch monitor never noticed. It wasn't until about two hours later that she mentioned it to her teacher, kind of as an aside. By then, it had already swollen considerably. She was okay, but we could not understand how such an injury did not seem to affect her in the slightest.

On the other hand, if she was only gently touched, she would cry out, and accuse whoever touched her of "hitting" or "punching" her. A slight tap on the arm to draw her attention away from the toy aisle generally resulted in, "Don't hit me!"

And she'd say it in front of whoever was present at the time.

Very loudly.

And repeatedly.

Followed by, "Yes you did!"

It's a difficult place to be as a parent.

This type of sensory impairment continued to cause all sorts of concerns at school. Clearly, any injury that requires medical attention is troublesome—especially if it is ignored. But the flipside is where Kristina continues to run into the most difficulty. Kristina frequently comes home from school, attesting that so-and-so hit, shoved, or punched her in line. The conversation often goes something like this:

"I am so mad at Sean! He hit me today!" Kristina exclaims.

"What? He hit you? Where? How?"

"We were standing in line, and he *hit* me!"

"Did the teacher notice?"

"I told the teacher, and he did nothing! Sean told the teacher he tapped me on the arm because I was talking in line. But it didn't feel like a tap. He *hit* me. I *know* he did!"

"Were you talking in line, Kristina?"

"Well, maybe, but…"

"Was Sean in charge of the line today?"

"Well, yeah, but…"

"Are you *sure* he actually hit you?"

"Well, he touched me really hard when he tapped me on my arm, and it felt like a hit, so he…"

Case solved.

In this example, Kristina translated Sean's touch into a hit. Just like one of us patting her on the arm for her attention in the toy aisle.

Another scenario revolves around Kristina being the declared instigator. Those scenarios usually go like this:

"Kristina, what is this note in your binder about bothering a student in line today?"

"Mrs. Substitute is so unfair!" states Kristina.

"Why? What happened?"

"She says I stepped on Janey's feet, and I didn't. I didn't even touch her!"

"Are you sure you didn't accidentally bump into her?"

"No, I never touched her."

"Kristina…"

"I was turning around to see who was behind me, and then Janey told Mrs. Substitute that I stepped on her. She is such a liar!"

Just like the story in third grade, "Misunderstanding the Rules," where truth resided on both sides, truth resides equally here. In this fabricated example, Kristina stepped on Janey when she turned around to look behind her. Kristina was oblivious to the sensation of stepping on anything different. So, to Kristina, she did not do anything wrong, as she did not notice stepping on anything (anyone). Still, she is at fault.

It is easy to see how inappropriate translation of sensation can cause a host of problems. Couple that with the inability to "think it, not say it."

Life in our household is never dull.

Ever.

Except for a pair of old scissors, and my only paring knife.

Meanwhile, Kristina frequently comes home sporting bandages from paper cuts, which rarely even bleed. We are becoming partial to the sparkly ones.

I am thinking of donating a case of them, in her name, when she graduates from elementary school.

This is where Occupational Therapy has made the most difference of anything, thus far. Kristina still struggles with spatial proximity, and other sensory issues, but her attention to strong sensation is beginning to awaken.

Occupational Therapy was fourth grade's silver lining. Mrs. Kim worked with Kristina on a weekly basis, and provided us with tools to use at home. At first, we were skeptical. When someone hands you a rectangular plastic brush, and tells you to brush your child to calm them down, it seems, well, a bit strange.

Especially when you consider you are to use the brush on their arms and legs, not head.

And it's a brush meant for corn.

The brush is nothing compared to your daughter telling you that they zipped her up from head to toe in a bag, with no arm or leg holes.

And how much fun it was.

"But don't worry, I could see out of it and breathe just fine!"

Mrs. Kim held an OT workshop shortly after Kristina began receiving Occupational Therapy services. We were unable to get a sitter, so asked if Kristina could join us for the meeting. Mrs. Kim did not mind, and even asked Kristina to be the model for the meeting. During the meeting, Kristina bounded all over the room, obviously running her engine at full steam. We felt frustrated, as Kristina wanted to do anything but play quietly. However, her activity was fine with Mrs. Kim, so we told ourselves to relax, and follow her lead.

Eventually, she called Kristina over, and demonstrated the Wilbarger brushing technique, along with joint compressions. Kristina happily complied. She went from full throttle to half speed in a matter of seconds—right before our eyes. It was as if someone flipped a switch. Mrs. Kim excused her, and she went about her business at a much calmer pace. If I hadn't seen it for myself, I wouldn't have believed it.

It is important to note that we were trained in the proper usage of the Wilbarger Protocol, and joint compressions. Such therapy should not be applied without the proper training and tools.

Another tool Mrs. Kim showed us was a small inflatable cushion. She suggested we use it on Kristina's chair at the dinner table, as it would help her stay seated, something Kristina had never before done. She mentioned that some students use these cushions on their seats in school, in order to help them to sit still at their desks. Seeing as the brushing technique worked so well, we were game to give the cushion a shot. It was a cheap solution if it worked, and if it didn't, we'd only be out a buck.

Later on, we could not find the type of cushion shown to us, but found a small inflatable ring, which did the trick. I remember the first night we tried it out. Kristina wasn't fidgeting. She wasn't half-standing, half-sitting. She wasn't complaining about the inflatable, squishy seating arrangement, either. In fact, she loved it. She was in her chair, *seated* and focused for all of dinner. This was another first.

Before we left, we asked about the body bag.

Apparently, the bag has a name: the Body Sox™.

The Body Sox™ is an elongated, stretchy bag that closes, encasing the wearer from head to toe. Although it appears opaque from the outside, those using it can breathe in it, and see out of it. It helps the wearer with her sensory processing disorder—finding her "place in space."

It also looks pretty cool to a fourth grader.

Rumor has it that the Body Sox™ is very popular at Kristina's school.

Kristina gave us a demonstration before we left.

I wish I had brought my camera...

The cushion, Wilbarger brushing technique, and other tools really, truly worked. From that moment on, we were sold on OT.

One day, as I was chatting with a friend of mine, I mentioned the cushion's success. She sounded quite interested, and decided to try it with her son during their upcoming visit. Unfortunately, I neglected a key component in our conversation—the size of the hole. Her son was younger, more petite than Kristina, and his bottom fell right through it.

You live, you learn.

Hope Kim was the very first person at school who truly seemed to understand Kristina. She believed us when we told her that assemblies and such bother her. She even explained why. She taught us which limits to push, and how far to push them. A very approachable person, we told her our concerns with the school and lack of understanding regarding our daughter's Asperger's. An incredibly bright individual, she helped us to discern which concerns were due to Asperger's, and which weren't. We now had someone we could truly rely on to help others in the school understand Kristina. Simply put, we had our first in-school advocate for our child.

We were overjoyed.

Hope Kim truly opened our eyes to the neurological reasons behind many of Kristina's behaviors. As a result, fourth grade served as an awakening for many of Kristina's senses. Kristina, like many others with Asperger's, has Sensory Integration Dysfunction. Our daughter went from stepping obliviously on objects, to saying "ow" anytime something touched her skin. At first, we thought she was merely looking for attention. It seemed odd, as she is an only child, and seems to get attention when she wants it.

Then it clicked.

For the first time, she's noticing these things touching her, and isn't quite sure what to make of it.

We started teaching Kristina as though she were a very young child. We started to let her know when certain bumps and scrapes were no big deal, and when others really needed attention. We tried to be matter of fact, not discounting what she translated as pain, no matter how insignificant the boo-boo. After all, to Kristina, slight pain is still pain. Our job is to help her determine the severity of each situation.

It's an ongoing process, but she seems to be learning okay. Still, there are times we'll notice a boo-boo she acquired during the school day, and she'll have no clue how it got there. There are others where slight contact will result in tears. She still flails away with most light touches from anyone. Meanwhile, we find ourselves collecting more glances from others who see our daughter cry over every little nudge and scratch. The older she gets, the longer the glares.

The tougher our skin needs to be.

Our focus remains on Kristina, not someone else's opinions. Kristina is making progress, which is significantly more important than my feelings, so, for now, we will do our best to ignore the stares.

One benefit to OT has nothing to do with Kristina or school. It has everything to do with my husband and I as parents. Much of what we struggle with as parents can find its answers in OT. Family members have chastised us, saying we are the reason Kristina hates hugs. Others have complained that we baby her when it comes to sound, although she is very bothered—to the point of tears—by certain types of sound. OT showed us that certain sounds actually cause her pain. Kristina has a hard time finding herself in space, which contributes to a host of other problems, like standing in line. OT has taught us that there is a neurological reason behind her lack of spatial awareness. This list goes on and on.

No, we are not perfect, but OT has let us breathe, and focus on our daughter, without spending countless hours trying to defend our parenting or questioning it ourselves. Simply put, we had more pieces of the puzzle, and a glimpse at the picture on the box.

OT isn't an overnight success, but it has opened wide a door to the sensory world we felt would always be opened just a crack.

As fourth grade unfolded, Kristina resumed social skills training, but this time with the school psychologist, along a few other fourth graders. Kristina referred to it as "Group." Working with the psychologist (the same one she had in third grade) was a welcome change from Kristina's prior social skills experiences. As it turned out, contrary to our initial assumptions, this psychologist is a very competent, caring woman. She was simply wonderful to work with.

We received a weekly sheet from Group, simply listing what they worked on, as well as a smiley or frowny face, depending on Kristina's attitude in Group. The sheets also helped us talk with her about what she learned that day. It was simple, yet offered a wealth of information, as well as a useful tool for home. It took a very small bit of effort on the part of the school, but conveyed what was necessary, just the same.

We don't ask for much, just to know where we are on the map.

Or even a peek at the cover of the puzzle box.

Even with OT and Group, fourth grade had me begging for summer break for the first time in all of Kristina's education. It even had me consider home schooling, which is something I've never pictured myself involved with. My husband and I strongly feel that Kristina needs the social interactions that school provides. In addition, my husband and I figure that if Kristina goes through school without one challenging teacher, it would be astonishing. We're hoping she's "paid her dues," and that the next would be a better fit. After all, difficulties are life's great teachers.

Our struggles in fourth grade did not revolve solely around Kristina's classroom experiences. At times, Asperger's would rear its head, and, like Lucy, we'd have some 'splainin' to do ourselves.

One day, Kristina came home and said that Mrs. Fourth Grade tried to put her in a group with Bob and Garrett. She said she told Mrs. Fourth Grade that we do not allow her to be with Bob. She held firm, and ended up working on her own—which, of course, made her content.

Kristina does not like group work.

We were petrified.

We never told Kristina she could not participate in group work with any of the other students. Ever. We e-mailed the teacher, telling her we did not say that. What we did tell Kristina was that we wanted her to stay away from Bob—at times like recess and free time. This child's behavior was the basis for our concern, along with our daughter's lack of social perception and spatial awareness. According to Kristina, Bob was aggressive, hurting students at recess, and saying some pretty nasty and threatening things to others, including our daughter. (In defense of our daughter, we were able to confirm some of her claims.) We were concerned she would antagonize this student, and become injured herself. (Again, being the communicator she was, we never did know whether she believed us, or saw us as controlling, disagreeable parents.)

Looking at the situation, we did not think to clarify to Kristina that teacher-assigned classroom groupings are exempt. We learned the hard way that "stay away from" means many things to us, and only one to Kristina. Kristina was not able to differentiate between the two. We should have known better.

Oops.

Toward the end of fourth grade, we found ourselves back down the same old hallway, seated at the same small table with Mrs. Fourth Grade. This time, the OT and school psychologist were present. The purpose of the meeting was to tweak Kristina's 504 plan for fifth grade. Overall, the meeting was a success. Afterwards, we profusely thanked Mrs. Kim for her understanding of Kristina, and for all of her help and support. She, in turn, confirmed to us another one of our suspicions. Some educators are supportive when it comes to Sensory Integration Dysfunction, while others are reluctant to honestly consider it. This was another pink pearl picked up along this journey. It is one we're keeping and remembering with each new teacher we meet.

Sometimes, when life seems to rest on solid ground, a layer of earth falls out from under your feet. As she had on the last day of third grade, Kristina stomped up the driveway, mad as a hornet. She had not been assigned to the popular fifth-grade teacher's class. Once again, the popular girl got the very teacher she wanted. Instead, Kristina was placed with someone unfamiliar, in the process of transferring to her school.

Andrew and I were not as dour. Kristina was finally going to be in class with her best friend. Her only true friend. Her heart's friend, Emma. We figured it couldn't get too much worse.

We were right.

PINK PEARLS

for Chapter Four

FOR THE CAREGIVERS

. . . .

Go in order

Suspecting trouble in the classroom? Communicate with the teacher first, before proceeding to contact the principal—not the other way around.

Stick to the facts

Be prepared to approach the school if the situation warrants. Be sure to gather all the factual information you can before you meet, as well as keep an open mind during the process. Although, unfortunately, some situations are truly detrimental, some difficult situations are simply a result of misunderstanding.

Advocate for an advocate!

Keep an eye open for an in-school advocate for your child. This person should be someone who not only has a solid understanding of Asperger's, but your child as well, as Asperger's presents differently from person to person.

Asperger's in Pink

The stranger it is…the better?

As long as therapies are within the realms of safety (psychological, as well as physical), consider letting the professionals give them a try—no matter how off the wall they may seem. Some of the most effective therapies seemed the strangest—like "brushing."

Remember to say "Thank You"

Be sure to thank those professionals who have helped along the way. It's all too easy to complain, especially when life is overwhelming. Make the choice to be an encourager, and thank those who are beams of sunshine along the way!

Look at the bigger picture

As tough as things can be in the moment, try to look at it from a perspective of time. Will this difficult situation be a learning opportunity, or is it truly serious enough to warrant intervention or even significant change?

FOR THE EDUCATORS

It's all about style

Certain teaching styles, while effective for many, may, indeed, border on detrimental to the young Aspie sitting in the classroom. With that in mind, be sure to create the best teacher/student fit possible, being willing to change it, if necessary.

Consistency is crucial for credibility

Don't set a rule you aren't willing to consistently abide by. For instance, if you don't allow drinks in the classroom, don't have one sitting on your desk. One of the quickest ways to lose credibility is via double standards—even in the "little" things.

Protect the student

If you observe another educator disrespecting or discriminating against students, or have strong reason to suspect such, be proactive, and speak with the proper administrators. It's the right thing to do.

Communicate, communicate, communicate... with a smile!

Repeat: communicate, communicate, communicate... with a smile!

Workshops are wonderful!

If possible, provide an after-school workshop for the caregivers, demonstrating to and educating them in current therapies. Consider allowing the super-special child to be present as well, as they can serve as a practical example.

Sensory Integration Dysfunction is real.

Join a group! Social skills groups are wonderful tools for kids who struggle socially. Those that meet during lunch provide a double benefit, as kids tend to be more relaxed then, and do not miss out on instructional time.

Asperger's in Pink

FOR EVERYONE

. . . .

An old adage is still a good adage

Actions always have, and always will, speak louder than words.

I WISH

. . . .

More parents had shown up at the OT workshop.

INSIDE the
BUBBLE

The Parent-Teacher Conference

Holding our breath, we waited for reality to set in. Surely, the ball would drop, the curtain would part, and we would learn that Kristina wasn't succeeding, after all. Just as in first grade, when all seemed fine, then BOOM, we prepared ourselves for another blow.

As with the past five years, we awaited the fall parent-teacher conference with the usual twinges of anxiety. We had the routine down. *Hi. How are you? Please have a seat. Kristina is very bright. She's a straight-A student. She won't look at me when I teach. She has trouble with the other kids. She can't accept ideas that are different from hers.*

"Kristina is a joy to have in class" never rests on our ears.

It's been tough.

Andrew and I kept busy while we waited for our turn, looking over the same few pieces of classwork posted in the hall, just outside the classroom door.

As I tried to stifle my urge to pace, I regretted the fact I did not schedule the sitter for more time.

As the young teacher finished up with another parent, my heart leapt. I could feel my face begin to flush. No longer on deck, it was our turn to bat.

Relax. Smile. Speak slowly. Listen.

But as we sat down at the small table, a relaxed smile crossed the teacher's face, making us feel at ease. He genuinely seemed happy to see us.

After years of parent-teacher conferences that focused primarily on our daughter's behavioral concerns, and which left us feeling belittled or inept, this one focused on *Kristina*. This one focused on who *Kristina* is, what works for her, and what she needs to work on. This one focused on her future, and how to get her there. It was all about Kristina. It was not at all about this problem or that. It was truly about seeing Kristina for who she is, and how to work with her to get her to be the best she can be.

It was the first conference I left smiling.

Ever.

Walking down the carpeted hall, I even smiled out loud.

Andrew glanced at me, wondering why I was laughing in the hallway. Being the type of person he is, he chose to focus on areas Kristina needed to improve. He wasn't sharing the moment.

Put another way, from days of old, he was killing my buzz.

He seemed to be interpreting my joy as ignoring Kristina's struggles, but that wasn't the case at all. After sharing with him my perspective, he managed a smile, too. Oh, how much better this year already seemed over the last!

Aside from the frustration of the latest school psychologist suggesting Kristina be reassessed, potentially having her rock-solid-iron-clad diagnosis overturned, aside from the reality of other skeptical school personnel looming overhead, Kristina finally has a teacher who gets Asperger's. Who gets her. Who may even become her newest advocate in the school setting.

What a relief.

For the first time, we may have a taste of respite.

For the first time, I felt what it was like to have a "normal," low-stress parent-teacher conference.

It took only six years.

But it could have never come at all.

As I continued to walk back down the hallway of the elementary school, I glanced at Andrew. I couldn't help but smile out loud again.

"Six years! Finally!" I said.

This was our last parent-teacher conference in elementary school. And it was an Ace.

In many ways, this report card was not much different from those before it. I haven't worried about Kristina's academics since her first year. Her consistent struggle is in the social sphere. Kristina's social weaknesses were indeed noted on her report card. They came as no surprise. As in the past, they echoed her Asperger's. What lightened my load was the attitude of the teacher.

Mark Williams did not speak to us in a confrontational manner. He did not talk down to us. I did not feel like I was sitting in the principal's office, in trouble. I felt like a respected parent. He had points he wanted to make, and he made them. He had concerns to share, which he did in a non-threatening manner. He couched some concerns in the context of future thriving in the school setting. He painted a bigger picture for us, for Kristina, and it all made sense.

Simply put, he gets it.

And he is looking at Kristina in light of the far-away future. Her future.

For the first time ever in Kristina's academic journey, an *educator* understood it all. It was such a relief. For the first time, I felt like a "normal" parent, whose kid is performing adequately in school. I did not feel judged. I did not feel like my child is a burden to the school. I felt there is genuine concern for her, with an approach focused on *Kristina*.

I walked down that hallway, smiling, with a bounce in my step. For the very first time, I left a parent-teacher conference...happy.

I felt that I had been given the stamina needed to weather another winter in North Shore. I can't imagine a better teacher for Kristina at this point in her life. As much as I wanted to leave here, I could now see myself tolerating this place for a few more months for Kristina.

Just Kristina. Simply Krissy.

All I can think of is how much ground Kristina stands to gain over the next several months. She is doing so much better internalizing her frustrations. She is happy again. She goes to school without complaining. She comes home with a bounce in her step. It's as if last year's load has finally fallen off. It's as if this year is blowing a warm summer's breeze, with the scent of my grandmother's rose garden in the air.

Even so, change will happen, no matter where we lay our heads. Kristina will be out of elementary school, out of this building. Change will arrive by September. The small brick building, traded for a larger, unfamiliar place.

I saved the reminder slip for the conference, keeping it with her first quarter report card. It's just a simple slip of paper, maybe 3x4 inches in size, roughly cut. By itself, it's hardly scrapbook worthy.

But, it's been six long years in coming. It's a day I never thought I'd have. A conversation about my daughter filled with *hope* and *understanding*. Sure, Kristina has areas to work on, but don't we all? Is there really such a thing as normal?

Chapter Five

The Teacher Who "Gets It"

Optimism vs. Pessimism

MOM: *"Kristina, when you see a glass filled to the middle line with water, would you say it is half-full or half-empty?"*

KRISTINA: *"Well, of course, it's both. It's half full AND half-empty!"*

Sometimes I think we are making great strides. Other times I think we live in a sinkhole. The stress can be overwhelming. From time to time, life on the surface often does not reflect life below. By September, Kristina found herself not sitting in the class of a transferred teacher, but a long-term sub. When we learned over the summer that her teacher was on an unexpected leave, more gray sprouted. The revised plan called for the sub to teach until the regular teacher was able to return.

Great. It takes half the year for a teacher to get to know Kristina. And this teacher seems young, so must not be very experienced. This should be fun.

All I could think of was how the teacher would spend a few months getting to know Kristina, then leave, with the process repeated once the permanent teacher returned. I could not see how that was a good formula for success—for Kristina or the school.

It is inevitable that new teachers will arrive on the scene each school year. However, finding out that your child will have one teacher for the first part of the year, and another for the remainder was tough. Especially when your child takes a long, long time to adjust to the beginning of each and every year.

At least she was placed with Emma once again. We did our best to encourage her to have a positive attitude about it all. No one seemed to know anything about either teacher, which made Kristina anxious. This was tough for Kristina, although after last year, Andrew and I remained optimistic.

As school ramped up, we were able to meet her new teacher before the first day. Kristina managed a smile as we walked out of the classroom toward home. "He didn't seem *so* bad," was all Kristina admitted.

As school began, it took Kristina several weeks to return to her old self. Summer break wasn't long enough to do the trick. The first week or so of school, Kristina continued as usual, with a smidge of crankiness and sarcasm, still not back to her pre-fourth grade self. Midway through September, she began to walk up the driveway with a bounce in her step. Cries for home schooling all but disappeared. She began to smile again. She returned to her old chatty self. She liked her teacher, and it showed.

It was as if Kristina had to see for herself that school could be better before she could regain her trust. Even though her new teacher seemed pleasant from the start, it took a few weeks in school for her to believe it. Once she let go of that anxiety, she was able to relax, and let her old self shine through.

To us, her teacher seemed warm and bright. Kristina was happy. She was learning, enthusiastically sharing lessons at home with us.

It was marvelous.

It was also maddening.

We knew the behaviors and sarcasm of the previous year would take a while to overcome, but we did not realize how deep and widespread the erosion to Kristina's self was.

Early in the year, I met with her fifth-grade teacher, in an effort to speak with him about Asperger's and Kristina. As this was only a temporary assignment for him, I entered the meeting quite skeptical. But when I walked into the room, I couldn't believe my eyes. I had read all about visual controls in a classroom setting. This was the first time I could truly see them, and they were all over the place. Things were coded not only by color, but also by shape. He posted schedules prominently at the front of the room. Everything seemed to have its own, organized space.

He happily explained his system. I asked him where he had gotten the idea, thinking it must be the curriculum, a new teaching program, or even the system of the other teacher.

He said he had come up with this system on his own.

It was simply amazing.

He also had information about Asperger's on the table in front of us. He admitted this was the first time he had heard of it. However, he had gone through it before the meeting, read up on it, even marking passages he wanted to discuss. He mentioned areas he felt did not apply to Kristina—and was correct. He mentioned areas where he could see fitting Kristina—and was also correct.

He focused on Kristina, not our family.

For the first time, Kristina garnered all the attention.

Finally.

As the weeks went by, her teacher decided to use a sticker system to communicate Kristina's behavior at school. A sticker meant all is well. He used a note home to indicate otherwise. This called for minimal time on his part, and was a quick reference for us. That is all we have ever asked for. Just a simple thumbtack on the map, which helps us balance Kristina's struggles with the school's perspective. It's easy, quick, and effective, much like the Group sheets sent home from Kristina's social skills group. We have never asked for a daily dissertation on Kristina's behavior and attitudes, just a rough idea.

Her teacher also quickly learned that humor goes far in diffusing Kristina, unlike harshness or sarcasm. Later that fall, at the parent-teacher conference, he gave examples of how Kristina reacted inappropriately, and how he was able to turn the situations around. This was something he discovered all on his own.

Simply put, he got it.

This teacher, relatively fresh on the working circuit, got it better than some of the previous teachers, with years and years of experience. This teacher, simply a long-term sub, proved more effective and understanding than many seasoned professionals did. This teacher focused on teaching and understanding, fully viewing the situation at hand, as opposed to settling for preconceived notions, or the previous influences of others.

It blew my mind.

The proof of his success lies in Kristina. Kristina was happy again. Kristina looked forward to school. Kristina was enthusiastic about learning, and her grades remained high.

But that wasn't the best part.

The sky turned blue, the sun appeared, and doves flittered on the air as a double rainbow graced the sky. Tree branches waved happily with the autumn breeze.

Okay, maybe that's being a bit overdramatic. Simply put, life took another turn, the road smoothed and straightened. The long-term sub turned into Kristina's yearlong teacher.

Sometimes, respite does come. Sometimes, we *can* sit, rest, and breathe.

It's amazing how many more miles you can travel after a quick stop to refuel.

Although Kristina's classroom experience flowed smoothly, fifth grade did not proceed flawlessly. Weeks upon weeks of the school year going swimmingly, we ran into black ice.

Twice in one week.

Black ice is invisible, always impossible to anticipate. Some of the worst winter accidents happen as a result of it.

Kristina's anxiety over the first assembly of the year overflowed, causing her to have her first outburst of the season. And it was a doozie.

Assemblies are a continual source of anxiety for Kristina. They are a shift in her routine, bringing displays of the unknown with loud sounds and sometimes shifting lights. This particular assembly had a reputation for being loud, even among the adults. Increasingly worrisome thoughts of sitting through the presentation proved too much for Kristina. According to her teacher, her anxiety was evident before she even entered the gym. After crossing the threshold, Kristina discovered that holding her ears shut was not as productive as using her legs.

She bolted out of the gym as soon as the assembly began.

Down the hallway.

Away from the teachers.

Tears streaming down her cheeks.

The caseworker followed suit, grabbing hold of Kristina, most likely in an effort to protect her and stop her from running away, as well as bring her back to the assembly. To Kristina, the caseworker came across as irritated. She recalls her telling her something along the lines of being in trouble, making Kristina feel even more upset. Kristina resisted returning, her anxiety increasing. Luckily, the psychologist also tracked her down, and convinced the caseworker to allow Kristina to spend time with her during the remainder of the assembly.

This small act eased Kristina's anxiety tremendously, and demonstrated sensitivity toward Kristina's sensory world.

Although everyone, including us, did their best to remind Kristina that it is dangerous for her to run off like that, our pleas were ignored. To Kristina, the assembly was overwhelming, and she needed to remove herself. She knew she was simply going to the bathroom, and was not going to leave the school. She could not see how adults responsible for her could not know where she was headed. To Kristina, they should have known she would not choose such an irresponsible action.

Or, in Kristina's words, "I would never be that stupid."

We could not get through to her. Her perspective superseded our concerns and rules.

Then came library day. The librarian chose to read selections from an author, some of whose work we do not admire, as it is visually upsetting to Kristina. Her lack of ability to take a broader view reared its head. We assured her we did not want the school to compel her to read some of this author's works, referring to specific, gruesome examples that we felt would be over the top for Kristina, and which Kristina was terrified to read herself. However, we did not make a blanket statement. *Some* of her works are perfectly fine with us.

Kristina being Kristina, we might as well have made our intentions a whole cloth quilt. She refused to listen to any benign work from the author in question. She argued with the librarian, in front of her entire class, stating we would not allow her to read any books by this individual.

Period.

Unfortunately, much like the incident involving Bob and Garrett, Kristina misunderstood our intention, and would not bend. Her rigidity was in high gear. The result was a show of disrespect towards the librarian.

And a call home for us.

And a letter in her file.

And yet another phone call.

In truth, Kristina was standing up for what she thought were our family's values and rules. In reality, she misunderstood our directive, disrespecting the librarian in the process. She did not have the social skills to adequately handle the situation, or interpret our guidelines.

This series of events precipitated a call from the caseworker, as the new psychologist (Kristina's third) was only in the school part-time, and that day, she was out. True to form, her first action was to question our family's personal life, asking if anything had changed at home. She did not focus on Asperger's or Kristina's Sensory Integration Dysfunction as the root cause, even though I implored her to. Because both outbursts had occurred within the same week, we were immediately suspect. This conversation with the caseworker was equally upsetting as previous ones.

I wanted to vanish.

Thankfully, Mr. Williams called to touch base with us. He explained his perspective on the week's events, and we talked through it. He gave me an objective view, and a much broader picture of the situation. As was his style, he focused on Kristina. Fortunately, we had already had several communications with him before these episodes occurred. This allowed him to know us, and us him, before any problems arose. As a result, he seemed able to divine our intentions, our insight into the true cause for Kristina's anxieties, unlike the case-worker. In the end, he helped calm us down, leaving us the ability to once again breathe.

Still, it was hard.

I have yet to find any upside to black ice.

Before his call, I started researching Asperger's schools. Even with the understanding from Mr. Williams, the calls from the school had me near the end of my rope. If Kristina was going to continue down the road of misun-derstanding, then maybe the best thing was to pull her out of the public school setting. In a stroke of luck or God's grace, I stumbled upon Dr. Stephen Bauer's (1996) article, "Asperger Syndrome". The section entitled, "Thoughts for Management in School" resonated with me. It underscored that many of her behaviors (her responses to negative stimuli) during that time should not be compared to her neurotypical peers, but in light of her Asperger's. In fact, Dr. Bauer stated in his article that, "Too often, behaviors in these children are inter-preted as 'emotional,' or 'manipulative,' or some other term that misses the point that they respond differently to the world and its stimuli." It was a fresh wind under-neath my weary wings. Dr. Bauer's article has proved to be another wonderful resource for us.

Another journal entry explained my emotions during that time:

> *I feel like I just got socked in the gut, but now I am putting the gloves back on. Reluctantly so, as I'd rather never pick them up at all. But I have*

to. I am a fighter, though not by choice. And I have to fight—for my daughter, for my family, and for all the other Aspies that follow after her. So, I'll take a few deep breaths of this nippy fall air, gather myself, my thoughts, and proceed with determination. If only the day would come when this fight will end, and I can live in peace. It is as if there are either little blips continually along the way, or a smooth run, followed by hairpin turns. Fortunately, the call with the teacher went quite well. He tried to look at the whole picture, and appeared very level headed. For the first time, save the times speaking with the occupational therapist, I felt our family was understood. The more people we have who understand all the dynamics, the easier I can breathe. The better off Kristina is.

Thankfully, those two outbursts were the only outbursts all year.

Still, we had difficulties. The revolving door of school psychologists continued, with Kristina's latest assigned psychologist in the building on a very limited schedule. Early into the year, she suggested that Kristina's testing be repeated, as she felt her Asperger's diagnosis was incorrect. Not only did she suggest retesting, she pushed for it.

Quite firmly.

At that point, she had only known Kristina a month or two.

For less than one hour per week.

As I pressed her for information as to why her diagnosis was in question, I received no response, other than "updating the testing." But Asperger's is something Kristina will not "outgrow." It is who she is. Her request for testing did not make sense to me.

I asked her about her experience with children who have Asperger's. She had plenty. I asked her about her experience with girls who have Asperger's—the same question I had asked last year's psychologist. She'd had none.

I strongly recommended that she speak with Kristina's pediatrician or therapist before pursuing any such testing, mentioning that I would not agree to any such testing without prior consultation between those individuals and the school.

I even pulled out the school budget card. I commented that speaking with those professionals might, indeed, save the need for retesting—along with saving the district massive amounts of funds needed for such.

Immediately after that conversation, I contacted Kristina's therapist, who reassured me that Kristina's diagnosis was, indeed, firm. She also mentioned that she could put something in writing for the school, or perform a retest, if the school remained insistent.

Not long afterwards, the push for any retesting concerning her Asperger's diagnosis ceased. Only routine, updated testing was performed.

Unfortunately, although the psychologist is a well-intentioned woman, she allowed Kristina's Group schedule to become sporadic, which did not sit well with Kristina. In fact, Kristina began to speak negatively of her. When I spoke with her about her attitude, she said it came down to the fact that the psychologist "didn't keep her promises" (keeping Group at the same time, on the same day), and kept changing or canceling Group without telling her ahead of time.

It all came back to unexpected change, and changes in routine. Something Kristina struggles with, and something quite typical of someone with Asperger's. We spoke with her about Kristina's trouble accepting such a schedule, though things remained in flux.

On a positive note, the school psychologist had us looking toward middle school, making sure we had some understanding of the process there, as well as suggested services for Kristina. She wanted to make sure that Kristina's 504 plan was reviewed, and tweaked for the big change. She did a wonderful job helping us to understand the special education process—better than anyone else had up to that point. It is always refreshing to work with someone who looks at the present in light of the future.

And, for the first time, she suggested Kristina begin work with an autism specialist as middle school gets underway. With Kristina's lack of an internal navigator, we were relieved that the psychologist had secured several hours of such service for her.

Beyond school and special services, we tried to do what we could to prepare Kristina to be independent. As Kristina heads towards middle school, and even life on her own, Andrew reminds me I need to give her more rope. He's right. Still, knowing when to do so isn't always obvious.

One cold, February morning, I decided to seize an opportunity to do just that. Kristina had her hands full of things to bring to school, and asked for a ride in. I scraped the snow off the car, while Kristina buckled herself in. We parked in the small, secondary lot, along with a few other parents. Every other time, I would walk Kristina to the cornerstone, before setting her free to find the rest of the way herself. Over the years, I had noticed much younger kids plodding up the side streets, unaccompanied by their folks, successfully, and safely, making their way into the school building. Today was Kristina's turn.

After encouraging Kristina to go on her own, I sat for a moment, making sure she was safe. As I watched her walk away, I noticed she headed in a new direction—toward the main parking lot—and traffic. Quickly, I opened the car door, and shouted her name. Kristina kept moving along. As fast as I could, I left the car, keys, pocketbook and all, and ran toward her, shouting her name as she moved farther into the main lot, into the bus loop. Kristina did not notice my calls to her until I was approximately ten feet away from her. Even then, I had to physically steer her toward the side of the building. The look in her eyes was slightly distant, perhaps overwhelmed. A quick "I love you," and Kristina was among the other kids, walking into the building.

I could feel my mind shake as I headed back home. Kristina, with middle school only a handful of months away, still needed help navigating. I was shaken. Over five years of attending the small school, periodically walking from the small lot to the cornerstone did not register on her mind. Instead of choosing the familiar path, or even choosing to follow the masses, she chose her own path—right in the middle of a busy parking lot.

Once home, it all hit me. With all of the strides we've made over these several years, the reality that she has autism smacked me squarely in the face. As much as Andrew *is* right, and I do need to give her more freedom, I also need to remember this: always be on guard.

As I was pulling a small filter for my morning coffee, the phone rang. It was Andrew, just checking in. As I told him what happened, he reassured me; he comforted me. The timing could not have been better. *Thank you, God.*

I've heard that people with Asperger's can and do live successfully on their own. At times like this, I often wonder how Kristina is going to get there. I wonder when she is going to get there. The thought of her making her way around a congested middle school building leaves me feeling hopeless. I can't help but wonder if next year will bring a new aspect to special services. I wonder if she will need an aide—not for the classroom—but for navigation, for more than just a few hours with the autism specialist.

On the whole, we were very pleased with our daughter's elementary school. Sure, it was not perfect, but neither are we. Hopefully, these early wranglings with the school will help as she moves on to middle and high school. Hopefully, we have shown ourselves as a family trying to work with the school, educating ourselves about the process and Asperger's, also concerned about our daughter's educational future. Only time will tell.

One of the most difficult aspects of this journey has been the feeling of being misunderstood, and under a microscope as a family unit. It is one thing to hear an educator verbalize their basic understanding of Asperger's. It can be quite another to see the actions that follow those very words. When an educator tells you they understand, and then questions and complains about the very behaviors that echo Asperger's, you lose faith. All we can do is show the school our efforts, and a spirit of wanting to work with, not against, it.

Still, being an objective parent is often like pulling the sauce off a spaghetti noodle.

Having a teacher like Mr. Williams, and a specialist like Mrs. Kim at the school have done nothing but help Kristina grow and prepare for life. As my daughter's peers ramp up typical middle school behaviors, these individuals are providing her with the tools she'll need to function along the way. We are forever grateful for them.

Meanwhile, like a warm sunny day in early September, I can't help but feel a bit sentimental as elementary school comes to a close. All too soon, the days of Valentine parties, Fun Fridays, and other things, will end.

Today, I will resist the urge to dwell on the future, but consider the present, who is just about to get off the big yellow bus, bouncing up her long black driveway, home.

PINK PEARLS

for Chapter Five

FOR THE CAREGIVERS

The sun does come out tomorrow

No matter how hard it is in the moment, grab on to optimism as tightly as you can. Keep looking toward the sky, and eventually you will see a beautiful rainbow, be it in the form of a teacher, therapist, or family member! Journal the beneficial times, so you can look back when the clouds roll back in.

Use your advocates

If the school questions your child's medical diagnosis, have both the medical and school professionals speak with each other. The result may, indeed, call for updated testing. However, it might negate the request for it, and spare your child from having to repeat it.

Give her room to move!

Make a conscious choice to stretch your child's level of responsibility, but stay nearby in case the opportunity is more than she can handle.

Consider volunteering

Many schools encourage parental involvement. If you are able, volunteering is a good way to further connect with the school, as well as provide the school an opportunity to get to know your family better.

FOR THE EDUCATORS

Stickers are super!

As communication is key, yet time is often short, consider using a simple sticker system, number system, or even smiley-type faces to communicate regularly with home, using notes for more pressing concerns.

Consistency is crucial

Although teachers are expected to change from year to year, it is very difficult to approach each school year with a new school psychologist. It takes a long time for trust, as well as knowledge of the child to be built. Please, whenever possible, try not to reassign these professionals.

A little reading goes a long way

Even if the caregivers overwhelm you with a cart full of information, take some time to become familiar with not only AS, but the strengths and struggle points of that student. Often, a quick conversation with the parents, school psychologist, or even previous teachers or the OT, can be beneficial.

Asperger's in Pink

FOR EVERYONE

Keep the focus on the kid

What are her current struggles? Strengths? Where is she headed a few years from now? Is she on the right path, or does she need to be redirected? Look at the child in light of her future. What is the best way to help her now to reach future goals?

Look at the glass as half-full

We were wrong to assume how school professionals would understand and react to our daughter, and Asperger's. Since then, we've learned to give the benefit of the doubt, first. Caregivers need to be careful to resist the urge to judge educators based on their apparent experience, or seeming lack thereof. Likewise, educators need to resist the urge to judge the family first, and ask questions later. Looking optimistically at life is simply a better way.

I AM THANKFUL FOR

A certain 5th grade teacher, who taught more, gave more, than anyone else, and who has bestowed a lifelong positive impact on one little, super-special girl—and her parents.

SECTION THREE

Community

INSIDE the
BUBBLE

Trying to Teach Empathy

Evening came, and Andrew was back home. Good news is a good thing, and he'd have some tonight.

"How was the dentist today, Kristina?" he asked.

"Mommy, you tell," said Kristina, looking toward me.

"But, honey, why don't you tell him?"

"Because I already told you, and I don't want to say again."

"I really think you should tell him yourself."

Kristina glared at me from across the table. I returned the gaze, and Kristina spouted an answer. Kristina abhors saying anything more than once.

Finally, the visit to the dentist went smoothly. Andrew looked relieved, which helped me relax, as well.

"Did Mommy give you a prize today?" asked Andrew.

"Yes!" smiled Kristina. "Hey, Daddy, guess whose birthday it is today!" She asked, spontaneously off topic as usual.

"Um ... Noah's?" he guessed.

"No," said Kristina, smiling widely. "Guess again."

"Hmm ... McKenzie's?"

"No," said Kristina.

"I give up," he said.

"Keep guessing! Keep guessing!" she insisted.

"Oh, Kristina, I don't know. What about Stripes?"

"Yes, you got it! Say 'Happy Birthday' to Stripes!"

"Happy Birthday, Stripes. Kristina, how old is Stripes today?"

"He's eight."

"Wow, that's great!" said Andrew.

Kristina smiled, and bounded back to her room. She had a party under way for Stripes. Five other stuffed animals had been invited. Kristina had prepared well. A plastic container was used for the table, with plastic tableware and food carefully placed on top. Each animal wore a personally designed paper hat. Gifts had been carefully selected and wrapped in fabric scraps and old cloths. Kristina even took a picture. It was one heck of a party.

"Hey, Kristina! How's the birthday girl doing?" I called down the hall.

"Mommy, you know it's not my birthday today."

"Yes, I know, but your party is in a few days, so you are the birthday girl!" I said.

"Stop calling me that. It's not my birthday, so I am not the birthday girl. Geesh!" exclaimed Kristina, crossing her arms, and turning away from me.

"What kind of cake do you want this year?" I asked, trying to elicit some pleasant conversation with my almost-eight-year-old daughter.

"A doll cake, Mommy. You knew that."

"Yes, I knew that, but I was wondering what *kind*."

"Oh." Kristina paused for a moment. "I want the one with the sprinkles in the cake mix."

"Okay, so, did you decide who you want the doll to be this year?"

"Yeah. I want Lilo," answered Kristina, then she promptly left the kitchen.

That went well. I think it went well, but did it really? For someone enthralled with birthdays, she sure was too restless to discuss her cake.

"Did you buy me the wrapping paper I told you to," said Kristina, reappearing from her room.

"What? You like to pick out the paper you use for other people's presents. In the same way, it's up to the person buying your present to choose which paper to use for you," I responded.

"That's not fair!" Kristina protested.

"It's how it is," I replied. "It is very nice for others to buy you gifts. Telling them which paper to use is not very polite."

"So what?" responded Kristina. "They're just wasting their money if they buy an icky one."

"Kristina, you should be grateful whenever anyone buys you a gift, no matter what it is." I took a deep breath and continued. "Do you remember how to react if someone gives you something you already have? Or if it's something that you don't like?"

Kristina looked at the floor, lowered her voice and spoke, monotone, "Thank-you-for-the-gift."

"I'm glad you remembered," I said. "Do you want to practice getting something you aren't wild about?"

"Um, maybe later. I think I'm okay."

"Are we set with games?"

"Oh, yeah!" said Kristina.

"I think you'll have a lot of fun."

And with that, Kristina was off to her room, organizing another birthday party for her stuffed animals.

The presents from family surrounded Kristina as she sat in the small rocker I had when I was her age. She's growing up so fast. Sometimes, it feels as if she's growing up too fast.

Watching her open presents is always entertaining. I still remember the year someone had bought her a beautiful plaid outfit. She tore open the box, opened the lid, paused, pinched her fingers, grasping the least bit of material, slowly pulled the clothing out, and made quite a face.

"Ew! Why would anyone buy me this!" she protested.

There wasn't much use in explaining it to her. It was an adorable outfit. Just not to Kristina.

There are times we wish family were closer, like at birthdays. There are other times we are thankful they are not, like at birthday present opening time. The faces and remarks that have come out of that child's mouth can try the most gracious of givers. And, no, we don't let those remarks slide on by. Still, I'd rather work on the concept of thankfulness among just the three of us.

"Kristina, you got some really cool stuff," Andrew remarked.

"Yeah, I guess I did. I actually like all of it!" said Kristina. "Except the clothes part."

That's quite a compliment in Kristina language.

"Um, I'm a little hungry, still," said Kristina.

"Do you want more cake?" I asked.

"Cake?" questioned Andrew.

"Yes, cake," I clarified, "it is her birthday, ya know!"

"Well, that means I get some too," Andrew smiled, as he raced Kristina to the kitchen.

Chapter Six

Tuning In to Social Signals

On playing a feelings game:

PARENT: *"Kristina, it's your turn to pick a card."*

Kristina draws "lonely," and must show a face that expresses being lonely. Kristina smiles.

PARENT: *"I've got it! Happy!"*

KRISTINA, SMILING: *"Wrong! It's lonely!"*

PARENT: *"Kristina, don't you feel sad when you are lonely?"*

KRISTINA: *"No, I feel happy! I like to be alone!"*

Kindergarten was a year of fun and learning. For Kristina, who thought she knew everything, and didn't need school, Kindergarten meant birthday parties. At Kristina's school, the customary practice was to invite all girls to the celebration of the birthday girl. The same seemed to hold true for first grade. Second grade came, then third, and the parties began to wane. Fourth and fifth grade arrived, with only one invitation at the beginning of either year. Then it happened.

The party train stopped.

On some level, we expected this. Still, we hoped things would be different. Somehow, Kristina would miraculously acquire social skills, and the partying would continue. I am grateful for the ones she was able to attend, but my heart aches for her, for the many she never was, and never will be, invited to.

Fifth grade has proved to be the most difficult regarding Kristina and peers. A few new students, wanting to prove themselves, decided to chop down Kristina, and a few other kids along the way. Kristina's quirkiness became fodder for them, as well as a handful of other peers, wanting to climb the ladder of popularity, needing someone to step on along the way. Although the academic and special services component of school was solid, the social component crumbled. Cries for home schooling resumed, as a spirit of nastiness invaded her otherwise pleasant elementary school experience.

It was crushing on all accounts.

Watching your daughter bloom in October, only to wilt in the spring is unbearable. With lots of encouragement, and prayer, we are getting her through.

Setting all political correctness and niceties aside, I'll call it like I saw it. Many of the popular kids became bullies, plain and simple. But isn't that often the case? Thankfully, another girl chose to stick by Kristina, despite being teased herself for being Kristina's friend.

Enter Emma.

Emma has been a patient, funny, tolerant friend to Kristina. I can't imagine another like her. She has been an oasis in the social storm of Kristina's childhood. The fact that Kristina really doesn't have many friends used to upset me greatly, and I remembered a prayer I uttered a long time ago. *Please, Lord, just one good, solid, real friend for Kristina. Please.* Then I realized He had provided that friend—Emma. *Thank you, God.*

Unlike all the other kids, Emma laughs at Kristina's jokes. They both share a love of princesses, while the other girls consider royalty passé. Emma has a high tolerance for bluntness, and will call Kristina out if she controls too much of the show. Simply put, they clicked. To date, this relationship has been the only one that seems to go both ways. It is a jewel.

Kristina has had minimal success with a few other kids. During fourth grade, Kristina was somewhat included in a trio in her class. Two other girls allowed her to join them for group projects, lunch and such. Neither girl tended to contact her outside of school, so I'm not sure how much of a two-way street it was. Nevertheless, inclusion is inclusion, and she got a taste of it that year. Not many names, but a few gems worth more than a bucket full of acquaintances.

As the years pass, we have seen the gap between Kristina and her peers increase. In some ways, I don't really mind. At least that's what I tell myself. Our family is fairly conservative, and I really don't mind not having to struggle with telling my daughter she is not going to a party where all kids under twelve are watching a PG-13 or R-rated movie. I like the fact that she has no interest in pop stars, or certain scantily clad plastic dolls better suited for the red light district than the pink aisle. I like how she thinks they dress "inappropriately," and wants no part of that. She still has a sense of innocence, and I, for one, am in no hurry for it to up and leave. Middle school will take care of that soon enough.

Another girl in her class has similar feelings, so Kristina has not been alone. Still, the days of knowing she's a bit different have, unfortunately, begun. On a positive note, she is finally beginning to sense these social signals. A skill that is intuitive for most children has begun to grow in Kristina. That is a good thing. Even so, it comes with a price. Fourth grade was the year where Kristina began to notice her peers purposefully leaving her out. She seems increasingly able to pick up on times other girls want nothing to do with her.

It's a heartbreaking place to be as her parent. It's also a heartbreaking place to be as a child. Still, it is encouraging that she is developing a sense of social awareness.

In light of all this, our goal is to help Kristina through these years, to help her envision adulthood, and to focus on future success. We try to help her look at the end of the road, not the speed bumps along the way. But in the here and now, that thinking does little to lessen the immediate sting. Meanwhile, we remain thankful for Kristina's one solid, heart-level friend, Emma. I hope, for Kristina, that she and Emma will always stay connected on that heart level. It is a gift I would give Kristina, if I could.

As Kristina embarked on experiencing social omission, I assumed my husband would understand it all. I assumed he would innately know how upsetting it is to sit alone here or there, while other kids congregated. But he didn't. Apparently, most guys can pick up from one group or person, and move on to another without as much thought. As I didn't grow up around many boys, his take on it was a novel concept to me. Likewise, the thought that Kristina was miserable because she was left out at recess was novel to him.

The reason I bring this up is to point out that boys and girls are generally different. Both girls and boys with Asperger's are probably more likely to be omitted from a group than not. However, I believe the emotional toll on the girl *may* be stronger than for the boy.

Or at least more misunderstood.

This does not mean the boy isn't bothered. In fact, the boy may receive more physical bullying than the girl. However, the emotional bullying girls can dish out is rather nasty and long lasting; more psychological than physical. My hunch is that girls may internalize their hurt to a greater degree. Yes, both the boy and the girl do hurt. Years of such social omission and hurt are bound to harm the psyches of all of these kids. However, my guess is the harm is *collectively* greater in girls than boys, as girls handle social situations differently to begin with.

Some people think that Asperger's is akin to a more highly evolved male brain. An article written by Carlin Flora, entitled "The Girl with a Boy's Brain" (published in the Nov/Dec 2006 issue of *Psychology Today*) touches on that subject, stating that, "…some scientists conceive of them as expressions of extreme 'maleness'—a talent for systemizing as opposed to empathizing." For the boy, this makes him eccentric. For the girl, not only is she eccentric, but she is walking around with a way of thinking, of processing information that is altogether different than her female peers'. She's already starting out on the wrong foot.

Add to this the social pressures of how we "see" boys and girls. In spite of the various women's movements, much of society still places great emphasis on how girls should look and act. Even neurotypical girls feel the societal pull to conform to certain images. A while back, I read a book entitled *Reviving Ophelia,* written by Mary Pipher. The author did a terrific job discussing just that—social pressures and assumptions placed on adolescent girls. Couple this with an Aspie's basic struggles, and one can imagine how much more confusing fitting in can be for a girl.

Or how strong she needs to be to truly live up to be who she feels she should be.

Then again, as I have a daughter with Asperger's Syndrome, perhaps I am biased.

When it comes to social interactions, it would appear that Kristina would naturally be more closed to adults than her peers. That's not so. In fact, to Kristina, adults are no different than kids. She treats them all the same. Although there are many times I think she benefits from being an only child, there are a few times where I can see it doesn't help. I wonder what her mindset would be if she had a sibling and saw that sibling also having to go to bed early, and speaking to adults in a different manner than her friends. I wonder if that would give her a greater understanding of how to react appropriately to adults. In reality, it probably wouldn't make much difference. To Kristina, they are all people, plain and simple. They either do or don't deserve her respect. They either do or don't pique her interest. She either does or doesn't want to interact with them. Age has nothing to do with it.

Interaction with peers has never come easy for Kristina. We often look for extracurricular activities to plug her in, looking for something to stick. We tried to get Kristina involved with Girl Scouts, but the local troupe was full, with never enough interest to start another. It was suggested to us to look into a social group for kids Kristina's age with Asperger's, but where we live, there aren't any. The only group we could find was geared toward older kids. The kicker was that her therapist—who runs the older group—was the one who encouraged us to find such a group. Yet she had no resource for what she recommended.

This is why I am turning gray quickly.

Ask Kristina; she'll confirm it.

Loudly and proudly.

In the middle of the pink aisle.

Andrew and I looked all over for all sorts of opportunities for Kristina. One day, while Andrew was reading the paper, he ran across a listing of the American Girl® book club to be held that weekend. It was worth a shot. Kristina adores the American Girl® dolls and books. As almost all of the girls in her class claim they have no interest in them, we thought this would be a good way for Kristina to share her interest with other girls. Kristina was thrilled with the idea. So were we.

The first few meetings went off without a hitch. Then life took another one of those hairpin turns.

One particular meeting, very few girls showed up. Kristina claimed a seat at an empty table. When Kristina got up to check some books out, another girl sat in the seat right next to hers. Upon returning to the table, Kristina decided that wouldn't work, and quietly picked up her things and moved to another empty table. We were distracted, and didn't catch what she had done until moments later. We were embarrassed. We did discuss the situation with her, and tried to help her understand how she made the other girl feel, and why the other girl's feelings were important.

But Kristina didn't get it.

Her motives for going to the club were quite different from ours. She simply wanted to hear about the books, and participate in the activities. She had no interest whatsoever in meeting new girls. In fact, she wanted to sit alone. We repeatedly tried to explain to her how her behavior upset the girl she moved away from. We tried all angles. We social storied like crazy.

Kristina stood firm, un-empathetic.

In Kristina's world, she wanted to be left alone during the club meeting, and that was that.

It's odd to consider her attitude toward the girls at the American Girl® book club when you consider how upset she gets when she is excluded at school. Quite frankly, any interaction Kristina has with peers is a wild card. If there were a visual to explain it all, it would look more like a Jackson Pollock painting than a neat flow-chart. Like most things in Kristina's life, I think it all boils down to familiarity and control. Kristina had a different agenda for the book club, which was not dependent on other girls. School, however, is seemingly dependent, and she wants to belong. It's a case of the elusive social interaction combination lock.

I suppose the dreaded social realm will never be easy for her.

This is where I think Kristina does benefit from being an only child. I recall what a friend of mine, who is also an only child, once told me. She's always been excellent at making friends. She said that being an only child was her impetus to find and keep friends. I think, in her own way, the same holds true for Kristina. She does not have daily interaction with other kids at home, so she has become more receptive to that type of interaction. This desire of hers isn't constant, but I think it encourages her to try harder than she would otherwise.

Still, Kristina's unique approach to life often hampers the growth of her social circle.

And, to some extent, ours.

When you have a super-special child like Kristina, you get to know who your friends truly are. As has been said, it's much like separating the wheat from the chaff. A casual invite to a fireworks display results in so much anxiety for Kristina, tears and verbal worry pepper all conversation. Despite the fact that we have declined the invite, our daughter is riddled with worry until the event itself is past. Free tickets for a movie, ice skating show, or sporting event elicit similar, though less intense, reactions.

Kristina's difficulty with spatial awareness often brings its own set of issues, though she is greatly improving.

She can become so enrapt in play, she ignores all else surrounding her, including people and fine china.

While chatting with friends, it is not uncommon for Kristina to interrupt the conversation, interjecting something from left field. We may be deeply discussing the shrinking manufacturing base, when Kristina enthusiastically raises her hand, unable to hold her words in, exclaiming something along the lines of, "Ooo! Ooo! Did you know that my stuffed animals are having a birthday party tomorrow?!" Other times, she may be playing in another room, yet add to our conversation.

Often, her lack of volume control results in repeated, "volume down," along with the accompanying hand signal. Dinner invites often result in offending the gracious host, asking for something else to eat when she discovers an objectionable menu. To Kristina, pretty much anything aside from PBJ, plain pasta, and macaroni and cheese is objectionable.

That's boxed, all-natural macaroni and cheese, please.

Kristina has been known to exclaim, within earshot of the hostess, "What am *I* going to eat? I'm not gonna eat *that!* Don't they have something else I can eat?" Social stories help tone down such commentaries, but they have yet to quell them. As a dear friend of mine once said, regarding similar comments her child once made, "Sometimes, I just want to put a fork right in the middle of my forehead."

Figuratively speaking.

I think.

There are many reasons why our circle of friends is not as large as it once was. Truth be told, Asperger's is only a part of it. Most friendships Andrew and I have made have been either through his workplace or church. As his company has gone the way of many others in the 21st century, most of our friends have left the state to find employment. Some simply tired of the weather. Others finished their graduate degrees, also leaving the state for better opportunities. The result is most of the families we successfully connected with no longer live in the area, leaving us unsure how to shore up our local support base.

Friendships are like missing jewels, not easily replaced when gone.

Unfortunately, it wasn't always geography that separated us from our friends. Sometimes, it was their perspective on Kristina's behaviors, and autism, as well as our lack of skill explaining it.

For years, we had befriended a couple in town. We had Kristina, and they had their kids. As time went on and Kristina's lack of social acuity became apparent, our friends started viewing us with sideways glances. Once Kristina had her diagnosis, and we shared the news with them, the calls and visits came less frequently. Their perspective is that Asperger's is just the latest fad, and it's our parenting, not our child's wiring that is at fault. Slowly and quietly, we've let that friendship go. Thinking of it all makes me quite sad.

Even though we try to let people know how Kristina may react in certain situations, when push comes to shove, it can still be difficult. As her therapist once put it, some may misinterpret her rigidity as being spoiled, or oppositional. For the few who make the effort, as much as they try to wear a thick skin around our daughter, her directness, or evasiveness, can still be bothersome. (I submit this may be part of the reason her third grade teacher had difficulty not taking Kristina's actions personally.) In other words, Asperger's explains much of her behavior, but it does not excuse it.

Thankfully, most of our friends have been patient and accepting. Some have super-special kids of their own, managing issues altogether different. We have found a certain, unspoken bond with those people. We seem to have the most success with friends who have rambunctious sons. Still, it's been a long, hard road.

Truth be told, our shrinking social circle is not due solely to people choosing not to choose us, or folks moving, but also our choice to avoid potentially stressful and emotionally draining situations. So much energy is expended working with the school and other activities, that little is left over. Many times, evenings out are the furthest thing from what we need, which is relaxation and rejuvenation. We have even turned down opportunities to go out to dinner with other families simply due to the fact we are too drained to social story the evening away. It may not be the best of choices, but it is the one we have made.

Maybe I'm simply selfish.

As Kristina is getting older, we are trying to be more open to social situations. We go into each, with a social story in each pocket, along with a role play here or there. Then we take a deep breath or two, and head out, hoping our company will have patience and grace for the evening ahead.

I cannot stress enough how timid I have become as a result of even occasional negative remarks made by others. I know I need to grow a thicker skin, and keep trying. Andrew is right when he encourages me to let go, and worry less. Still, it is hard.

It continues to amaze me how life is full of double standards. Don't lie, but tell me my haircut looks good. Don't kiss up to the boss, but don't challenge her, either. Try to make deep friendships, but don't call me. Too many one-way streets, or drives down lonely roads, only to turn around time after time. Iron sharpens iron, though iron left alone turns to rust. Simply put, it's a circular scenario, with a downward spiral. You need social interaction to work on social skills. Poor social skills limit social opportunities.

Even so, we continue to search out opportunities for Kristina to develop appropriate peer relationships. We are not giving up.

Just as in our dealings with the school, we need perseverance, patience, and prayer to make it all work.

PINK
PEARLS
for Chapter Six

FOR THE CAREGIVERS

Make room in your heart for hope

Watching your child miss out on so many "typical" childhood pleasures of play-dates and parties is very difficult. However, current situations do not necessarily dictate future ones. In other words, do not assume your child will never make that one good friend, or never attend a party.

Be thankful in the little things

An "everyone's invited" party is still a party. Resist the urge to compare your child's social calendar with anyone else's.

Know your child's agenda

What is the impetus for your child and socializing? Boil it down, and approach "making friends" with her vantage point in mind.

There are two sides to every story

Keep in the front of your mind how your child interprets life. Her interpretation of social situations may not accurately reflect them. Use each as an opportunity to help her learn.

Separate the chaff from the wheat

When a friendship loses its roots, it's time to move on.

Don't give up!

No matter how tired you may be, keep searching for, and trying on, new social opportunities for you and your daughter.

FOR THE OTHER MOMS

Be present at the play-date

If your child has a play-date with a young Aspie, it's a good idea to stick around, and keep an ear open. Some *gentle* social coaching may be in order.

FOR EVERYONE

. . . .

Throw out the cookie cutter!

Do not expect girls with AS to mimic boys with AS. For that matter, don't expect girls with AS to mimic their neurotypical counterparts. View each child as an individual, and go from there.

I WISH

. . . .

There were more lunch monitors during lunch and recess, and that teachers were required to spend part of their lunch time observing the kids, even if only once per week, as most of Kristina's bullying occurred then.

ॐ

INSIDE the BUBBLE

Holidays are Hard

October is fraught with change. Sunlight yields to dusk. Warmth turns to chill, as white flakes start to ride on late October air. School is in full swing, and those of us residing near the northern shore prepare our homes for the long winter ahead.

Pumpkins and haystacks grace front porches, as orange and black decorations dot most yards. Alongside the celebration of the harvest, October holds Kristina's most feared holiday.

"Mommy, I'm staying home Friday," Kristina asserted, while taking off her backpack.

"Why?" I asked.

"I am not going to be there for the parade and all of that other icky stuff."

"I know you don't like Halloween. I don't really like it either. However, I can't just pull you out of school that day."

Kristina's anxiety was evident. Halloween, in Kristina's mind, has to be the most dreaded time of the year—even worse than getting shots from the doctor, or fireworks on the Fourth of July. So many costumes portray blood and other visually bothersome themes. The lack of princesses, animals, and angels is increasing among elementary school costume choices. Kristina is very much bothered by scary sights, and I can't blame her. They bother me as well.

It is hard to convey to those who are non-visual how such images can become engraved on your mind, and lie there for years. For those of us negatively affected by such imagery, shopping in October can be an unwelcome chore. Sights of death and gore peer around aisles of the grocery store, and bombard our senses, invading our dreams, even. Likewise, commercial breaks during TV programming. This imagery is an offense to those of us who are bothered by such. Each year piles on the last, and our anxiety levels, likewise, increase.

And religion has nothing to do with it. I know Christians who dress their children in the same gruesome manner as everyone else does.

I am at a loss to explain how American society searches out and celebrates the grotesque. These gruesome images are the results of actions we teach our kids to avoid: killing, torture, and the like. I have yet to hear a reasonable explanation for the acceptability of this celebration. Yes, my faith makes this time of year undesirable, but I could not tolerate those images even without it. Somehow, I cannot explain it all to my daughter.

My initial reaction was to pull Kristina out of school for that day, much like a few other parents we know. However, our job is to help Kristina learn to self-regulate in such situations, not place her in a bubble. Our goal for Kristina is to, one day, live on her own, successfully functioning in society. We need to help her get there now, not solely during her senior year of high school.

This was the last year for Kristina to participate in the parade. Her school is very parent-friendly, inviting the parents to be there, see their children in each and every parade. Reluctantly, my daughter marched along, her head downward, eyes focused on the carpeting. I have not thrust her blindly into those settings. We make sure she has supports. We make sure she knows that I, or some other trustworthy person, is there to help her if things become overwhelming. Just like taffy, she has to be stretched to grow. Just like taffy, it does not stretch itself, but is stretched, carefully, by others.

Kristina dressed up as Lilo this year. She beamed as she dressed like one of her favorite Disney characters. She even brought a stuffed Stitch along to complement her outfit.

As I entered into each room, alongside my daughter, I tried to take in the varied costumes of students and teachers. I smiled at some, and bit my tongue at others. Again, it's about choice, and freedom of expression, isn't it?

I remember Kindergarten. Kristina dressed up as an animal that year. We stood ready at the end of our driveway, awaiting the Kindergarten school bus, with costume in hand. The doors of the small bus opened, revealing a transformed bus driver. The fair-haired driver changed into a green-faced, dark haired witch. It was a bit much for Kristina. It was a bit much for me. The driver admitted her costume was a bit much for the young students, and apologized to us. I didn't know what to think. On the one hand, it was within her right to dress up as she saw fit. However, this particular bus is solely for the youngest elementary students, and scaring them before getting to school didn't seem like a wise decision.

This year's parade is bittersweet. It is her last, which means she is getting older. But it will be a relief for her to no longer be a part of this tradition.

We have never asked the school to outright condemn many of the outfits that Kristina finds bothersome, though we do make our opinions known. There are certain guidelines the school does establish. Although we could do without the entire experience, it is unrealistic to fight against it. I will save my energy for other issues—those known, and those yet to be known.

Kristina made it through the parade better than in the past. The evening brought another round of anxiety, though markedly less than the day. Andrew and I took turns handing out candy, and taking Lilo and Stitch around our neighborhood.

Kristina greeted our neighbors with a simple "Aloha" as she went from house to house with her pumpkin bucket. We rushed quickly down one street where ghoulish sounds blared loudly, setting Kristina off in the process.

Kristina longs to greet the trick-or-treaters, putting candy in their sacks, but the intimidating costumes of the few overwhelm her, so she reluctantly steers clear of our front door. In many, many ways, this holiday is a sensory stretch for her. It is for her mother, as well.

Soon, all is ended. We are thankful the weather held, and are thankful the day is done. Kristina's smile returned, and her stance relaxed. Two piles of candy cover the living room floor. One for her, and the rejects for her parents.

Sitting in the midst of her loot, smiling, Kristina announced there are only 363 days left until she has to go through it all over again.

Chapter Seven

A Part of (and Apart from) the Community

"If you think about it, what's the point of drying a swimsuit? Isn't the point of them to be wet?"

—KRISTINA, AGE 10

One of the hardest things about raising a child with Asperger's is the feeling that our daughter has something invisible. We have often commented that life might be easier for her if there was some outward indicator. In many ways, at first glance, Kristina appears neurotypical. If anything, her intelligence often has others assuming she is more mature than are other girls her age. However, her emotional "age," something much harder to discern, suggests someone younger. It's the old, old story of judging by appearance. It's also the old, old ending, of the cover not fully representing the book. It's another case of perspective.

Consider life. We all walk different paths, and have particular views on how it all unfolds. For Andrew and me, life is much like a day at the pool. Most folks are sitting by the side, wearing bathing suits simply for show, as they cannot swim. Some talk, others read, while still others nap. Several others are adept swimmers. These folks spend the day in the deep end of the pool, breathing through snorkels. Occasionally, these folks will come up for a brief stretch, though preferring to be fully submerged in the water's warmth. Both groups of people are clearly in the water, or out. We, on the other hand, spend the day in the shallow end of the pool.

We are breathing the air just as the sitters breathe. We are maneuvering in the same water as the swimmers. As our swimming skills are minimal, we settle only in the shallow end, merely waist deep. We take pleasure in the warmth of the water, while enjoying the touch of sunshine on our backs. We are more at home in the water than on deck, though the deep end is an area we will never fully explore.

We belong to neither group.

Or is it more accurate to say we belong to both?

Neither fully in, nor fully out of the water, we deem ourselves misfits. Our struggles are muted. They are not enough to warrant outward, obvious acknowledgement of the sitters. Most look at us, curious at to why we are in the water at all. Likewise, though welcomed in the water by the swimmers, many do not value our staying, as we do not seem fully equipped.

Such is how we view life in light of living with
Asperger's in community. In many ways, we move along,
living life much like the neurotypical. For instance,
Kristina is eligible to sign up for, and play, tennis and basketball, just like her classmates. We do not need special
physical supports for our home, nor do we require any
from the community. We know of people whose children
will always need diapers, and who may never be able to
live without an aide. Kristina has been in a mainstream
classroom, so far without an aide. At the same time,
Kristina's Sensory Integration Dysfunction, lack of Theory
of Mind, along with a few other odds and ends keep her
from fitting comfortably in the mainstream.

Suffice it to say, life for us is a little bit different.

Early on, so much of our time was caught up learning
the ropes in regards to Asperger's Syndrome, the school
system, and so on. There was little time to simply sit
and soak it all in, and little energy for much else. Eventually, life slowed down, leaving us to see our daughter
in a whole new light. After all, life does not consist solely
of home, school, and the doctor.

Or even a pile of Asperger related books sitting atop
long lists of websites to check out.

In order to thrive as a family, we need to get out of
the house from time to time. We need to interact with
other people. As Lucy once said to Charlie Brown, "I
know what you need...you need involvement." We
need to live in community.

The twenty-first century is not wanting regarding
things to do, places to go, and little guy soccer. If anything, the average life of your typical elementary school

child is rather hectic. For us, it wasn't a matter of finding things to do, but the right activities for Kristina. When looking into sports, we chose ones that leaned toward developmental versus competitive. We prefer inclusive activities, versus exclusive.

This does not always sit well with our daughter.

I guess one could say we are being overprotective. Some may sermonize to us the benefits of competition. We contend that Kristina will experience such soon enough. For us, Kristina's involvement in sports is not about winning, but about being part of a team, working with a group, and personal benefit. (On an honest note, Kristina's gross motor skills, though improving, are not strong, compared to her peers.)

Consider soccer. In our town, soccer is quite competitive. Kristina played two years in the youngest leagues, which were considered purely developmental. Even there we witnessed parents not only berating opposing players, but screaming criticisms at their own children as well. As the age of the players increases, so does this sort of parental behavior. In our area, there is much emphasis on winning, and prepping kids for college scholarships, not so much teamwork or inclusion. To Kristina's dismay, we no longer sign her up for it. Simply put, it is not a healthy environment for her.

On the whole, Kristina's experiences with sports have been positive. And quite varied. She has participated in everything from tennis to basketball, with marginal successes.

Placing our daughter in sports left us with a choice: whether or not to tell her coaches about Asperger's and

Kristina. Over time, we simply found it best to watch, wait, and see. If Kristina's sense of justice started to override the activity, or her sense of space became problematic, we told. The rest of the time, we sat on the sidelines, cheering her on.

Silently hoping she would keep her hands and criticisms to herself.

Kristina's participation in community sports went generally well. She tried. She showed good effort. Kristina being Kristina, sometimes she stood out.

One of my favorite memories is of indoor soccer at the Y when she was quite young. The gym floor was multi-purpose, with hopscotch painted in the corners. Sure enough, as Kristina ran to guard the net, she would become enticed by the hopscotch. The hopscotch won every time. As soccer moved outdoors, the tiny daisy-like flowers dotting the field took more attention than a group of girls running directly toward her. Now older, Kristina still fights to keep her head in the game, but she's improving.

Of all the sports Kristina has participated in, softball was a family favorite. Kristina's weak ball handling often frustrated her team members. But her coach had a different take. As Kristina stood in the field, seemingly oblivious to life surrounding her, she was thinking strategy. As other girls went for the homerun, Kristina was thinking of which plays would work best. Although her coordination was lacking, her effort was spot on. And her coach noticed.

Still, from time to time, Asperger's would rear it's head, and make Kristina stand out just a little bit. The

Asperger's in Pink

standard cheers the teams shared made her cringe. One in particular drove her nuts. Instead of looking at the cheers as a fun thing to do with her team, she took the words all too literally. One went this way:

> *We don't drink no lemonade;*
> *we just drink our Gatorade®*
>
> *We don't wear no miniskirts;*
> *we just wear our softball shirts*
>
> *We don't play with Barbie® dolls;*
> *we just play with bats and balls*

As Kristina's favorite drink is lemonade, and Kristina loves to wear dresses and skirts, this cheer ranked right up there with blasphemy. No matter how much we tried to explain the sentiment behind the cheer, Kristina declared her intent to show up at the last game in a miniskirt, holding a large bottle of the pink stuff.

Another time, at the end of an inning, Kristina noticed her visor was missing. She approached her teammates, asking them if they had mistakenly taken it. Before some of the girls could check, Kristina grabbed one off a teammate's head, to see for herself. It never dawned on her to rely on her words to find out. The teammate was obviously annoyed, and Kristina missed the social cue. We talked to Kristina about how she handled the situation, via a social story. At the next game, her visor went missing again. This time, Kristina used only her words, and it all worked out.

Aside from sports, our town has offered other family programs, and we have taken part in many of them. The recreation department of our town has done a great job of offering activities, such as egg decorating and a Christmas tree lighting ceremony, which have given my family many positive memories.

Just like other families with super-special kids, mainstream activities often suit Kristina just fine. Whenever possible, we want her to be able to learn and play in a mainstream environment. But just like other super-special kids, and Kristina being Kristina, sometimes, she needs another atmosphere. But how do we discern the difference between times to mainstream and times to get out of the stream? So far, it's all been by trial and error. This was the case with swimming.

Watching Kristina try to learn how to swim with a group of peers was discouraging. Kristina's lack of spatial awareness was quite evident, with her obliviously crossing into the paths of other swimmers. After three sessions, she could not doggie paddle, or even float. As other children progressed, Kristina remained stagnant. We knew something had to change.

The Continuing Education Department, which offered the typical swim lessons, also offered something called the Special Swim program. Kristina's Asperger's Syndrome diagnosis should qualify her for the program; however, we wondered if these classes were only for those who were more greatly disabled. We took a chance, and decided to sign her up for the class.

The first night of class brought with it a sense of anxiety. *Will people question her presence, judging her by her outward appearance? In so many ways, Asperger's is invisible. Will they think we are taking advantage of the program?*

Asperger's in Pink

Are we overreacting? We pulled into the high school parking lot, amid throngs of teenagers and hurried parents speeding from spot to spot. We made the familiar walk to the locker room, before finally arriving by the pool. Thankfully, a former instructor was there, and confirmed we made the right decision. In fact, this type of program was precisely what Kristina needed.

During the one-on-one lessons, an overall sensation of warmth and welcoming was evident. Judgment is not welcome here. We were among people who choose to look at souls, not faces. There was such a sense of peace, of acceptance. When Kristina screamed out, or refused to be touched, people did not glare in her direction or mine. We did not need to explain her quirkiness. You see, they've been there, too.

For the first time, it felt as if our family truly belonged.

It's all a matter of perspective, isn't it? We hear so much preaching on tolerance and acceptance. If only it would be encompassing. If only people would not judge too quickly. Still, it is hard to let go when so many years of sideways glances are imprinted on your memory.

The progress Kristina made during the first few weeks of Special Swim was no less than astounding. Her motivation to learn proved insatiable. It moves me to tears to see my child so energized to do all she can. She is competing against herself, and is proving to be a fierce competitor. She has a long way to go, but that's okay. As a former instructor once told me, all that matters is that she can right herself, and swim to shore.

My previous concerns revolved solely around whether or not Kristina was right for Special Swim. After years of participating in general community sports, we assumed swimming would be no different. We assumed she might have a blip here or there, but everything would work out in the end.

We were wrong.

This class is what she needs. It is what many other super-special children need. And it is working. Sometimes, it is good to put her in the mainstream. Other times, I found I needed to set pride aside, and take advantage of special classes and services. After all, it's all about what's best for Kristina, not my ego. It's about doing what's right. In doing so, we expanded our circle of community, and we are the better for it.

Aside from education and sports, we also try to cultivate the spirit.

For our family, community also involves church.

There are many reasons we attend church. We go in order to grow in our faith. We also go so we can be surrounded by others who share the same beliefs and values as we do. Church, to us, is the most important part of our community.

We attended a certain congregation for several years, believing it was the right fit. I suppose, at the time we made that choice, it was. The people were kind, and the teaching solid. Though many tried to understand Kristina, some got it, some didn't. Most struggled.

Kristina's reluctance simply to greet people made it difficult for any of them to feel like reaching out to her. Many who continued to try were often at a loss how to do it. In many ways, so were we. It's as if Kristina has a locked door to interaction with people. A very few people seem to hold the right combination to unlock that door. Once it's unlocked, Kristina's loosens, and speaks freely, almost non-stop. For everyone else, there is nothing but a cold, hard door. Sometimes, it seems as if she changes the combination.

For instance, there was one woman who was beyond kind in her interactions with Kristina. But Kristina continually chose to clam up on her. One day, Kristina brought a toy from her current special interest to church. When the kind woman was nearby, Kristina sprang to life, showing it off to her, bypassing any customary greetings along the way. Her actions were out of the blue, and somewhat disconnected, but it was a step. The next time she saw her, she avoided the woman.

Her actions confused us all.

We have yet to understand the secret for acquiring the elusive social-interaction combination to Kristina's special lock. We're her parents, so she gives us a pass.

Usually.

One particular Sunday morning, as a sermon unfolded, the pastor mentioned that he'd recently met a family that had an autistic child. He mentioned that he had never before met anyone with autism. Andrew and I sat there dumbfounded. He had known our family for years, and even Kristina's specific diagnosis, but, somehow, our talks with him never soaked in. From time to time, we assumed we were misunderstood. This man's words confirmed our suspicions.

That afternoon at home, we felt like pin-pricked balloons. As time goes by, I continue to believe that some people will choose to listen, but not hear, what Asperger's truly is. I believe that many people will always regard it as an issue of self-control and manipulation, nothing more. A few minutes here or there will not paint a full picture of my daughter, nor Asperger's, although many, many people acquainted with our family will try to do just that.

As always happens, things changed, and we changed. We felt surrounded by pleasant people, some of whom never really took the time, while others were simply too busy, to be deeply involved in our lives. With no family around, minimal supports in town, and middle school around the corner, we had a tough decision to make— to stay with the familiar, or make a change, and search for something better.

The likelihood of Kristina weathering life's storms with a strong support base at our church was weak. Looking as objectively as we could toward the future, in light of the present, we decided to look for another church.

Kristina was not pleased.

When I spoke with her about her honest thoughts, it mostly boiled down to change. She was familiar with the building and the people. She verbalized her desire to belong to another place, but could not work past the issue of change. Moving Kristina from point A to point B, knowing point B is a better place to be is much like unearthing an overgrown dandelion. The roots are deep, thick and seemingly unending. In order to fully remove the dandelion, much earth has to be dug away. If the root is not fully removed, the dandelion (problem) will reappear. It can be a tedious process, but necessary, just the same.

We needed to move on in order to grow. We had to remove ourselves. All Kristina could see was the beautiful yellow bloom at the end of the long, green stem. To put it bluntly, sometimes, Kristina needs help seeing past the bloom to the reality of the weed.

Just like the rest of us.

Sometimes, I believe that God leads you to a place for a little while, then picks you up, taking you somewhere unexpected. Through it all, we kept our eyes heavenward, having faith that God would place us where He wanted to be. And He did.

But that is a story for another day.

Although we strive to live out our faith, we want Kristina to believe because she chooses to, not because she's told to. We try to teach Kristina to understand that not all people follow the same religion that we do. Some people follow no religion. When we introduced the thought of respecting other people's religious viewpoints, we were met with a resounding, "Why would anyone believe *that*?"

If you think about it, your honest inner thoughts might sound similar. After all, if you claim your belief is true, then others will not be true. So, how can you rightfully embrace all other religious thinking if you fully believe yours is the one and only? In other words, when we teach our kids religion, we are teaching them that that way is *the* way. Therefore, someone, such as Kristina, calls is as it should be: Conflicting religions are wrong, and, therefore, the followers thereof are misled.

It all sounds rather harsh when put that way. I'd feel rather uncomfortable if my Buddhist friend approached me so bluntly. In turn, I would not feel comfortable going up to my agnostic friend, telling him the same. Still, do we "buy into" our religion or don't we?

Setting aside theological discussions, and focusing on pragmatics, her thinking should have us all thinking about our own beliefs. Do we truly believe what they teach? Are we willing to go to the wall for our beliefs? Are we uncomfortable believing, even sharing our faith? Even if the believing involves believing in nothing at all?

For Kristina, it's all rather black and white. To her, our religion is truth, period. Where is the inner struggle? Where is the embarrassment facing any awkward parts of our faith (if there are any) in the presence of others?

It simply does not exist.

She is convinced that her religion is right on, and she has a boldness that most of us lack. It does make many of us uncomfortable, but in many ways, it is to be admired. This way of looking at faith gets me thinking at a deeper level.

Early on, we were told that a good, *local* support base is a must. As much as we are involved in our local community, our support base is not as strong as we would like it to be. We understand how essential it is for families in our position to have others nearby to grow with and rely on. We believe that is true.

The problem is I can't seem to order one on-line.

Or upgrade our current base.

This foundation we need to build ourselves. This process has been an exercise in trial and error. We are very fortunate to have friends and family who are very supportive, though most do not live nearby.

Years of living life this way has us considering something we never gave much thought to prior to raising Kristina: moving closer to family. Now that Kristina has cousins, and middle school on the horizon, the timing just might be right. It just might be time to change our local community.

PINK PEARLS

for Chapter Seven

FOR THE CAREGIVERS

. . . .

Find the right fit

Try to take advantage of conventional community activities, but be open to looking into programs geared toward super-special children. Make sure that the goal of the activity (teamwork, gross motor development, competition, etc.) meets your personal goal for your child.

Realize certain holidays and celebrations may overwhelm

Blinking lights at the mall may enthrall some, but they can overwhelm others. Make sure your child has a go-to person for stressful sensory activities, such as costume parades and certain types of parties.

Watch, wait, and see

Choose wisely if or when to reveal your child's Asperger's diagnosis. Avoid the desire to inform others up front that your child is super-special. Be willing to let events play out first. In doing so, you will minimize the risk of singling out—or even embarrassing your child, and may find that your child rises to the occasion, and nothing need be said.

Keep in mind that her black and white view of the world extends to her view of faith

Regardless of your involvement in the faith community, consider teaching your child to respect different views. If nothing else, encourage her to keep her commentary at home.

There is more to life than home, school, and doctors

Examine your schedule. Are there openings for more family time? Community activities? Make sure your family is involved in something fun and life-building.

Put the ego on the shelf

Many kids with Asperger's have some difficulty with gross motor skills. In light of that, consider making enjoyment and development—not championships—the focus of any athletic opportunity.

Examine your community, and be willing to change it, if necessary

Do you have a wonderful support system in place? Celebrate it! Would your family benefit from a change? Consider it, and be willing to move on if necessary, realizing that your child will put up some resistance during the process.

FOR OTHERS

. . . .

Give the kid a chance

What a child may lack in ball handling might be made up in strategy. Have patience, and watch out for bullying on the bench.

Step up

Make sure that sensory-sensitive children have a person to go to when situations become overwhelming. Do not dismiss the child's anxiety in these situations.

Support the parents

Parents are often overly sensitive to their child's quirkiness. Help them feel at home by accepting their child—and them—from the start.

WHAT I'M THANKFUL FOR...

. . . .

The special swim program through the Continuing Education Department

⟨⊙⟩

INSIDE the
BUBBLE

Literally?

"It's only fair," I admitted to Andrew. "When I went to Hawaii without you, you did the same thing. You should enjoy any free time you get in England."

"I suppose you're right," smiled Andrew.

We exchanged good-byes as Andrew left for another work trip. Spending a few days with family in Cleveland paled in comparison to visiting ancient castles and standing on the grounds of Wimbledon. Neither of us had ever been to Europe, so it was difficult to hide my envy.

Thankful for blue skies and sun, Kristina and I headed west to spend time with family. As my husband traversed the Atlantic, we puttered along on the New York State Thruway. Somehow, it was hard to throw off the pity party.

My cousin Bethany's new kitten, Sally, made it easy for us to catch up on life, and her recent relocation. Eventually, Kristina's boundless energy proved no match for Sally. A new computer game highjacked her attention as we continued to visit, giving the kitten a needed break.

Though it was good to catch up one-on-one, I wanted to include my daughter in our conversations. As I walked over to her, I noticed her beautiful eyes surrounded by puffs of pink skin. It did not take long to find out that Kristina was allergic to Sally.

Thankfully, my cousin is a nurse.

After a dose of antihistamine, we got the situation under control, and instructed Kristina to leave Sally alone. Watch her, but don't touch her. Kristina was disappointed, but understood.

The next day, we awoke to more sun and warmth. Nurseries dotted the landscape, adding beautiful shades of green to a clear blue day. Bethany drove us around, and showed us their new neighborhood, eager to move in and move on to this next phase of life.

"These tracks are murder," Bethany said, as we approached a railroad crossing, obviously in need of repair work. "If I don't take these slowly enough..."

"They're going to *kill* us?!" exclaimed Kristina, from the back seat.

"Oh, no," answered my cousin.

"But you said they are *murder*," said Kristina.

Bethany chuckled, remembering how Kristina interprets language.

"Good thing I didn't bring up dead man's curve," she whispered to me.

Back at the house, we continued catching up on life, while Kristina enjoyed some down time. A few hours later, her fair skin once again puffed up pink.

"Oh, Kristina, are you touching Sally?" I asked.

"No, Mommy. You said not to, so I am not touching her. I promise."

Another dose of antihistamine went down the pipe, but Kristina did not improve much.

We were starting to worry.

As I sat in the dining room, thinking it all over, I watched Kristina play. Her love for Sally was evident, following her every chance she got. Kristina being Kristina, she came up with her own solution to spending time near the kitten.

Holding an arm cover in each hand, much like potholders, Kristina picked up Sally.

Though not physically touching her, holding her like that brought the kitten too close to her face. We now had the root of the problem.

"Kristina, when I said not to touch Sally, I meant not to pick her up."

"Oh. But I'm not touching her. That's why I'm using the arm covers."

Note to self: Next time, use an unabridged directive.

Chapter Eight

And Then There's Family

Kristina, age seven, on Thanksgiving: "What's the big deal about always having to have turkey at Thanksgiving? We always have turkey. Why can't we have something else, like pasta?"

"How do we explain this to family?" I asked my husband.

"They're not going to get it," he answered.

"But we have to tell them, don't we?"

My husband and I exchanged sighs as the reality of our daughter's diagnosis and the potential reaction of our extended family sunk in. The name alone was bound to cause a raised eyebrow from one relative, who continues to mispronounce it as "Ahhhs-berger's," as opposed to "Asss-berger's." All we could do was remain optimistic. We didn't know how extended family would react, though we could guess.

"They're going to think we're full of it," I said.

My husband gave me a look. It's at times like that I am glad we live far away from family. Somehow, we gathered our thoughts, our mode of address, and told family about Asperger's.

As with any other family, many were in denial, forming their own conclusions about Kristina's unusual behaviors. (A few friends of mine, whose sons have ADHD, confide similar feelings.) Most initially refuted her diagnosis, saying that Kristina didn't seem like those they read about who have autism. Others dismissed it, telling us how our parenting is the cause for her issues. (I bit my tongue on that one.)

With Special Ed teachers in the family, we had high hopes. Maybe they would have some grand insight, or connection for Kristina. Maybe their voices would resound with an "Oh! Okay, I know what that's all about. Now I understand why…" After talking with them, only one seemed to know about it, and that individual's knowledge proved limited. Unfortunately, we found ourselves in the strange position of educating the educators. To their credit, they performed their own research, in an effort to understand Asperger's. Since then, they have generously passed along various sorts of information, from books to articles to websites.

A few years have passed since then, and many of our family members now seem to make an effort to accept Kristina for who she is. It has been such a relief to see a relative's love and understanding evolve. This particular relative scolded me early on for defending Kristina's hatred of hugs. Now she passes on articles and other tidbits of information as she comes across them.

Another treats her like any other kid, and Kristina responds to her the best of any.

Unfortunately, we have found Asperger's hard for many people, including family, to wrap their heads around. Simplified, it all sounds like a bunch of incredibly smart people who have trouble making friends. In addition, being considered a high functioning form of autism, those like Kristina don't *appear* autistic, as others often visualize autism. It's an awkward place to be.

I wish I could say all our family accepts her for who she is. I wish I could say they see how hard my husband and I try to do the right things. But for some people, a closed mind is where they find their comfort. My job with regard to those individuals is to shield Kristina the best I can, equipping her with tools to handle these situations successfully. For instance, if relative BettyLou complains for hours about how Kristina didn't eat her sauce-laden meat medley with crunchy unidentifiable vegetables (and then ignores Kristina the rest of the visit), Kristina needs to know *we know* how she feels. We need to encourage her to hang in there, and suppress the urge to tell BettyLou that her parents choked over the same meal.

Despite mounds of ketchup.

Or, if relative RobbyBob isn't given a welcome hug, and then immediately explodes at her, we need to equip her with the means to psychologically handle his outburst and lingering grumpiness. Don't forget how to respond to relative BarbieJo when she gives her a button-laden, itchy wool sweater with the words "too hot to handle" on it, then has a meltdown because Kristina won't touch it.

Those examples are exaggerations, as are the names, but they paint a rough picture, just the same.

Here is an honest sampling from past visits: "You baby her too much," "It's your fault she's so picky," "Don't tell me that child doesn't like hugs. I'm family," "She is a manipulator. I have her number. Boy, do I feel sorry for you when she's a teen!"

Simply put, some people still think we're full of it.

After all, they are family, and the fact that they put up with us through puberty is apparently reason enough for some of them to consider much of what we say as suspect.

The majority of such comments stem from episodes where Kristina's sensory defensiveness comes into play. This often happens when family members want to hug and overwhelm with incessant talk and questions, then shut her off once they do not get a desired response. They want to engage Kristina on their terms, in booming, excited tones, which are exactly what distances Kristina from them. Then they want Kristina to sit quietly in the corner, reading, or coloring.

I find it quite ironic when family members look down their noses at our parenting style, meanwhile ignoring Kristina the entire time she's in the room. It is an awkward position we sometimes find ourselves in. In truth, such moments have strengthened us as a couple, even as a family. We look at the situation in light of the individual's behavior and attitudes, not "my family vs. his."

However, we seem to have found a common denominator to these troubles. Truth be told, we consistently run into difficulty with people who embrace an old-school sort of mentality. That seems to be the thread. On top of all this, there exists another great irony. Family members least empathetic appear to echo various markers of Asperger's themselves.

Family is not all rants. Sometimes, it is raves. Many have been tolerant, even heartening. Out of the myriad of family members we have, we are encouraged that some are successful in their attempts at understanding Kristina. In fact, one relative recently met someone whose child also has Asperger's. As a result of this woman's openness, my relative has developed not only a working understanding of it, but also an appreciation for it. Her patience with Kristina—and us—is a godsend. Her attitude truly lifts our spirits. Another quietly stands up for us whenever Kristina's quirkiness inadvertently rocks the boat of another family member.

When family accepts Kristina for who she is, understands that we are doing the best we can as her parents, we are able to more fully enjoy the extended family relationship. When they see areas of concern, and speak to us in love, we are much more open to listening, and are able to keep the lines of communication open. Not only do we have much we can teach them in regard to our daughter, they have much they can teach us, as well.

We have friends who have sons with some form of ADHD. They have experiences similar to ours. What I am trying to stress is the fact that relationships do change when you have a family member with something super special, such as Asperger's.

The bottom line is that it took time for family to understand and accept the diagnosis of Asperger's Syndrome Disorder. In many ways, for some, five or so years after the diagnosis, it is still taking time. Just as it is unrealistic for the school psychologist to create an accurate picture of Kristina in a handful of twenty-minute sessions, spread over a few weeks, so is it unrealistic for family to do the same when they only see her once or twice a year.

I'm not saying that Andrew and I will ever make Parents of the Year. We are far from perfect. What I am saying is that "the village" contributes to the growth or stagnation of all of us.

I truly believe much of life comes down to this: look at life from the eyes of another, and agree to disagree more times than not. This definitely applies to family. Ironically, years of social skills training are making my daughter more empathetic and sensitive than some neurotypical people, to whom such is intuitive, not learned.

We have found ourselves in the fortunate position, or not, of living at least a day's drive from the nearest relative. Moreover, these visits tend to be in their homes, out of Kristina's environment, as we end up doing most of the traveling. At times, it makes for a tricky situation.

Sure, there are pleasant benefits. We can come and go as we please. We can leave our home a mess. (Not that I would ...) There are no in-laws nearby to stop in unannounced, and analyze my housekeeping skills. (Not that they would ever do that ...) We can let the phone ring and ring, and no one will know if we are home or out. (Not that we ever screen our calls ...) We can pretty much live our lives our way.

Then there's the downside.

We are unable to participate in family parties, or watch our nieces and nephews grow up. Kristina is growing up with only a superficial knowledge of her relatives, which makes us all sad. Andrew and I both can't help but wonder if our relationships with our family would be more enjoyable if visits were more frequent, and less concentrated.

I had a sorority sister—yes, I will admit I was in a sorority—who was addicted to tanning beds. I recall a conversation I had with her about the appeal of those contraptions. I never did get the point, so I asked her what it was about them that she liked so much. She told me, in an effort to spur me onward to tanning bliss, the beauty of the tanning bed was the long-lasting effects after your time is up. She told me that, in her words, you continue to tan after the visit because your skin cannot absorb all of the light when you are there. She loved that concept. Accurate or not, that concept freaked me out.

The upshot of it all is that we spend most of our vacation time—and dollars—visiting our extended family. These visits usually last for two overnights, at minimum. Some trips are delightful, others a whirlwind. Then there are yet others. We often wonder if a few hours here beats a full weekend over there. Until then, family visits have the likelihood of remaining concentrated.

Sometimes, in all honesty, the process of visiting extended family ranks right up there with the fear of root canal work. Or a spinal tap. Or going through labor with no anesthesia. Trust me, as Kristina would quip, I've experienced all of them.

Okay, maybe I am exaggerating again.

But not about the labor.

When we travel to see family, we thrust Kristina into a different environment through which she has to find her way for days at a time. Kristina and change mix like oil and vinegar. The only way those liquids will create an emulsion is through constant, consistent, motion. It can be done, but it does not happen instantaneously—it takes perseverance, and time. Even the best of visits can be challenging for Kristina.

Visiting family means taking Kristina out of her environment, and her routine. Her schedule becomes flexible and unpredictable, which is not a good thing. Add to that trouble with spatial proximity in a home filled with breakables, and other fine things. Don't forget the menu, either. Not everyone has grape jelly in the fridge. Throw into the mix a long car trip, and, no matter how much we may want to see family, we are already starting out with a few strikes against us.

Along the way, we have discovered it is generally better to stay in a hotel, than directly with family. This initially caused hurt feelings on some parts, though it has made for much better visits on the whole. It is a pricey option, but has been well worth the effort. It has cut into our vacation budget, but, honestly, it has been better for Kristina.

When Kristina tires, her speed increases. When Kristina is out of sorts, she stimms. Kristina, like her parents, becomes easily overwhelmed when surrounded by people for hours on end. She needs a place to escape to have quiet time, something not easily accomplished when staying at someone else's home. Being away, with just the three of us, Kristina can be herself, and unwind.

And have a snack of crust-less PB&J—with grape jelly—at the end of the day.

Kristina being Kristina, the behaviors she uses to calm herself are, to the unknowing, odd, such as spinning in circles, or becoming excessively whiny or anxious. But consider how "normal" people behave under stressful situations. First, for the sake of argument, let's define stress for the purpose of this particular discussion. When I refer to stress, I am referring to the state of being where control over circumstances is unachievable. I am also referring to any such circumstance that will cause anxiety in an individual. Stress can be either good or bad.

Picture someone who has anxiety over flying. There are many different ways such a person will handle that stress. For some people, becoming chatty is one way of coping. Such a coping mechanism may be seen as friendly by some, and annoying by others.

Now, let's take that same anxiety, at the same level, and picture Kristina. Let's even consider she has the same coping mechanism: chattiness. Whereas the non-Aspie will go on and on about anything benign, let's picture what words Kristina's conversation would be replete with. Whereas the first individual may be thinking, consciously or subconsciously, that the plane might crash, or that someone will become sick on her lap, her conversation will not expose those thoughts. Kristina, on the other hand, may repeatedly vocalize such thoughts, at a high volume. "Are we going to crash? How do you know the plane is safe? Are you sure they locked the door okay? What if someone throws up on me?" She is thinking it and saying it.

It's the same anxiety with the same fears at the same level. The first person internalizes their specific fears, for whatever reason or reasons. Kristina is honest, direct, and vocalizes hers. What are the results of both expressions of anxiety? The first person is seen as annoying, at worst. Kristina, on the other hand, may be seen as inciting fear and anxiety in other passengers. This is not her intention, by any means. However, those actions are not socially acceptable for reasons that should be clear.

Applying this to a family visit, when tired and under stress, Kristina may vocalize all manner of things bound to upset. She often acts inappropriately. If Kristina becomes overtired and bored, she may reveal all sorts of things, such as how I told Andrew that Uncle so-and-so is such a chatterbox, and never gets off the phone.

Or what I really think of the pot roast we just had for dinner.

Or dictating tomorrow's dinner menu.

Our job as her caregivers is to search for ways for Kristina to cope in such situations, teaching respect in the process. Among other things we need to teach her are patience and grace.

Generally, we put it upon ourselves to watch her for signs she is beginning to melt. Meals can be off schedule, which makes a big difference with Kristina. We make sure we have snacks available in case dinner is running late. We also watch to make sure she is not going into sensory overload, or the converse—too little stimulus. We make sure she is engaged when she is open to social interaction, and encourage her to introduce her special interests to her relatives. We make sure she has down time during day-long visits, finding a quiet spot for her when she needs it. We also make sure we head out before she overtires.

For now, we are trying to stick with the hotel coping mechanism. It lessens Kristina's anxieties and frustrations, as she is guaranteed alone time. She can spin without worry. It also encourages proper behavior while visiting family, as she knows she will have some "off" time in the evening, if all goes well.

Truth be told, after going this route, quality time spent with family is improving.

Sometimes we wonder if attitudes would change if our family saw her on a regular basis. Probably, but there is no guarantee. In fact, moving closer to family may prove more stressful. Still, I've found myself lately wondering if we should uproot. We have some good services here, but are saddened by the fact Kristina is growing up with such limited experiences with her family. Deep down, we believe she would increase her enjoyment of her extended family if she saw them more frequently, in her environment. A few e-mails to my sister are helping me sort through it all.

Everything in moderation seems a better way to go, including tanning and family visits. For that reason, along with a few others, we are hoping to move closer to them.

It's funny. Life, that is. It seems there is always a cost to go from one place to another. Sometimes it's a bigger mortgage. Sometimes, it's more traffic or taxes. Sometimes, it's a loss of friends. Sure, there are often benefits outweighing those costs. The main concern I have in all of this is Kristina securing another relationship like the one she has with Emma.

But there is a price to stay as well, and it may not include their continued relationship. As time changes, so do people. The only sure thing is there is no such thing as a sure thing.

So what do you do? You count all costs the best you can, shoot a prayer up to Heaven, and take action. Even stagnancy is acting—to do nothing is also a choice.

For now, I'll relax, not worrying whether BettyLou, RobbyBob or BarbieJo will pop by unexpectedly tonight. I don't worry as much as I used to about what they think. My skin has grown thicker. However, I am human. The way individuals choose to react to my family does affect me. But I'm getting better at not dwelling on their negativity. I try not to obsess over what I can't control. I am also trying to look at my own faults, and honestly face up to them. I am also trying to put more effort into looking at the positives extended family brings to our life. Complaining is always the easy way out, but it is not the better way.

For now, I will choose to be thankful for those who accept our daughter—and us—for who we are.

And who love us just the same.

PINK PEARS

for Chapter Eight

FOR THE CAREGIVERS

. . . .

Determine boundaries

No matter how difficult it may be, this is the time to stand up for your child, and set healthy, reasonable boundaries.

Don't overwhelm

Make sure to provide adequate and appropriate information on Asperger's to extended family, but don't drown them in paperwork, or hyperlinks.

Unpack your pillow with careful thought and consideration

When traveling out of town to see extended family, determine the best place to stay overnight. It may not be with family, after all. Then again, it just might.

Don't play doctor...unless you are one

Despite the suspected Asperger's traits of Uncle RobbyBob, leave the diagnosing and referrals to the professionals. Use your hunches as an opportunity to understand him and better relate with him, not judge him.

Pack that extra bag!

If your child has a picky pallet, and only Grapey Grapes Grapeful Jam will do, be sure to either pack it—or bring extra cash to buy some—for your visit. Likewise other items, which will help keep your child afloat during the time away from home (and her routine!).

Remember respectfulness

Make a conscious effort to teach respect and graciousness to your child. Keep in mind that although Asperger's *explains* some of her (negative) behavior, it does not *excuse* it. Also keep in mind that it takes time, persistence, and consistency to instill such in your child. Don't expect an overnight success.

Be willing to uproot

Take honest stock of your support base, and other significant aspects of your life, and be willing to change it, even if it means moving hundreds of miles away to be closer to your family. Small bits of regular interaction with extended family really might be better than occasional, concentrated amounts. (And for some, the converse might be more appropriate.)

FOR EXTENDED FAMILY

. . . .

Determine boundaries

Just like the caregivers must do, it is also important to determine boundaries yourself. It is one thing to be flexible and understanding; it is another to allow children to swing from the very chandelier you hope to eventually bestow upon them.

Don't pass on the pamphlets!

It's not a bad idea to ask for information regarding Asperger's from the caregiver(s). Take a few moments to read up on it, and don't be afraid to ask questions about it, though try to keep those conversations out of earshot of the child.

Let the parents parent

But provide gentle, well thought out advice when you feel the situation warrants it, allowing the caregiver(s) the freedom to take it or leave it.

Respect the need for space

As difficult as it might be to learn your family will be staying in a hotel instead of your home, give it a try, without complaint. The nature of an Aspie is to need alone time, and spending time each day (or night) alone is one key to their success. In return, you may be pleasantly surprised with the quality of this visit, as opposed to previous ones.

Throw out expectations

Accept your family for who they are, not who you wish they were, and you will both enjoy each other.

ENJOY your family!

Some of the funniest phrases come out of the mouths of super-special kids, not to mention unique points of view. Make a concentrated effort to engage the child throughout the visit. Sit back, relax, and simply enjoy time as a family.

I AM THANKFUL FOR

...family members who choose to spend time and energy looking at life through smiles and giggles.

SECTION
FOUR

Day-to-Day

INSIDE the
BUBBLE

A Birthday Breakfast

"Welcome!" greeted the young hostess. "Three for breakfast? Please follow me," Her bright yellow shirt made it easy to follow her through the busy restaurant.

"Have a great meal," she said, arranging our wrapped silverware in place before heading back to the hostess stand.

Kristina's eyes widened along with her mouth.

"What?! A *table*? I'm not sitting at a *table*. Tell her to get us a booth!"

Here we go.

Again.

I quickly glanced around the room, noting a full restaurant. We were lucky to be seated right away. Tables aren't my first choice, either, but I knew we all needed to eat. The table would be fine.

"Kristina, we are not going to sit in a booth today."

"Why not!" she protested.

"There aren't any available for us right now."

"How do *you* know!" she exclaimed.

Great. Mental check. Only two tables worth of patrons are looking in our direction.

Wonder if Kristina will strive for three, or even five?

Breathe, Julie, breathe.

"Kristina, we are not going to discuss this any further."

Reluctantly, Kristina took her seat. Shifting all over the small wooden chair, she muttered and uttered all sorts of expressions of discomfort.

"Mommy, this chair is so uncomfortable! I can't sit in it."

Across the table, Andrew looked at me, with steam rising from his head. A sour look donned his face, while all I wanted was peace.

"I knew this was going to happen!" he quipped.

"That's enough," I muttered back to him.

"She's going to ruin this for you just like last year," he mouthed, ending with a deep sigh.

"Look, you can only control how you react to the situation. You are actually bothering me more now than she is," I whispered back. "You didn't even ask *me* if her behavior is bothering *me*."

"Is it?" he skeptically and reluctantly asked.

"No," I firmly replied, "but yours is. I can't calm both of you down."

Andrew relaxed, though ever so slightly. I seethed inside, as I felt I had to hold up three people—Kristina, Andrew, *and* myself. Sometimes I feel like the legs of a table. I often feel like the only one holding the family upright. When I crumble, the table falls. If I don't intervene, Kristina and Andrew might proceed down a path of terse words and tension. This is my birthday, and I'll be darned if I fall today—or hold the table up. He can play Atlas this time.

"Andrew, that's it." I comment. It was a risky move. Depending on how he interpreted my intent would determine how the morning moved forward. Still, I felt it worth the "risk." Let Kristina make all the negative vibes today. I wanted both of us to have a rest from the battle named "behavior modification" today. "Please stop. I need your support today," I implored.

Andrew sat there, water pooling in his eyes, looking blankly at the table. Poker is a game he could never play and win. He wears his thoughts on his face, with body language to support it. Although he is verbally keeping his thoughts to himself, I can hear his frustration shouting across the table, making it near impossible for me to relax.

Just one day off from conflict while eating out. Just one.

Please.

Slowly, and mercifully, breakfast arrived, Kristina's disposition shifting from cranky to pleasant. Chocolate chip pancakes solve a multitude of ills. We moved on to breakfast, as if nothing happened. Kristina sat bewildered as I shared bits of my meal with Andrew. In many ways, this type of sharing keeps us close.

Kristina found our habit perplexing.

And a little gross.

Even though we weren't literally feeding each other.

Truth be told, in many ways I should be grateful that Andrew was so upset with Kristina. Focusing on the negative emotions of the moment, I did my best to squelch all conversation, instead of looking at the whole picture. Andrew wanted me to enjoy my birthday breakfast. He wanted Kristina to behave like a graduate from charm school. He wanted me to relax and enjoy. He wanted the experience to be seamless.

That didn't happen, and it upset him.

I found all that out in the parking lot, after Kristina secured herself in the car.

And I felt bad.

I felt that I chose to see only one side of the story—his frustration with Kristina, which I took as ruining "my" morning. But that wasn't the case at all. I didn't do what I preach to Kristina. I didn't fully "listen" to Andrew. On a deeper level, his actions showed his love and care for me. Still, he admitted he needs to let Kristina's barbs roll off him. He needs to be Teflon® Man. Maybe someday, eating out will run seamlessly. Maybe someday.

In my quest for instant peace, I struck a nerve. I made him feel worse. But we are both making progress. The more we are matter-of-fact, the quicker Kristina's negativity shifts, and the better we both feel. In turn, the better we feel about each other.

That's a good thing.

Andrew is such a forgiving type, which I swear is why he sticks by me. Unlike so many others, he loves unconditionally. He loves to the end. He's persistent and loyal.

And there are days he has to remind me, too. See, I'm no saint.

Like life, so much of this boils down to control.

Self-control.

And knowing when to let go.

Thankful for blue sky, a warm winter day, full bellies, and my family, my birthday was off to a great start.

Chapter Nine

Holding the Marriage Together

About the song "Radar Love":

JULIE: *"Andrew, what does 'Radar Love' mean?"*

"Mommy," interrupting Kristina, "I think it means that he has to check the weather radar to see if he can go out on his date."

Ahh … the subject of marriage. The most personal of relationships. A subject worth noting. Two people, joined with the intent of being together forever. An emotional, spiritual and physical bond like none other. One that is as open to Aspies as to any other couple.

Marriage.

A topic I have avoided discussing like the Plague. Until now.

Not that I mind discussing marriage. Tell me all about a marriage, and sure, I can discuss it. I can tell you all about my sister and her husband. Or the man who is now with his third wife. Or the newlyweds at church. I can write easily about any marriage, provided I have the blessing of the couple.

As long as that marriage isn't mine.

You see, it's personal.

Somehow, though, it doesn't seem right to discuss our life as a family, and omit talking about our marriage. Somehow, all this digging deeper hits bundles of nerves and opens dark doors. It's not that we have a bad marriage, or a secret life. We don't. It's just that we are very personal people. If anything, we're akin to hermits. We don't even talk about our marriage with extended family. And, like many people, admitting any weaknesses therein is tantamount to abject failure.

Of course, that's not the case, and maybe we're even overreacting. No marriage is flawless. Of course, we make mistakes. Of course, we have imperfections. Of course, I do things that drive Andrew crazy. But that doesn't mean I want to write about them.

Or publish them.

Or flash them all over the Internet.

Still, the marital relationship needs to be discussed. Somehow, some way, I'll muddle through, and try to paint a picture of Asperger's and our marriage. Hopefully, it will resemble a Monet, more than a Jackson Pollock. But, hopefully, not as defined as an Andrew Wyeth.

Let's start with one of the basics. Having a kid together.

Having a daughter with Asperger's Syndrome.

At the moment, it is unknown what factors contribute to someone having Asperger's, though there are several theories. Currently, there is much discussion that Asperger's is genetic. Andrew and I have looked carefully at both sides of the family, and can see aspects of Asperger's on both sides. It helps us to understand our extended family and, in many ways, have greater patience with those individuals. Looking at family through an Asperger's lens also extends to the two of us. We often see bits in each other. We have often joked that we each share different parts, and, together, we make a whole: Kristina.

We are not sure if genetics plays the role, or merely a supporting role, but we both agree that it definitely plays a part.

Like many other parents, we are incredibly doting. Some might say we border on spoiling. (That assertion is simply subjective.) She is incredibly smart, talented, humorous and beautiful. (That assertion is clearly unbiased.) We love our daughter to pieces.

We're just like any other couple with a kid.

Kinda.

Sorta.

Just like many couples, we have a child who needs certain modifications, and who has certain life struggles. Unlike many couples, our daughter has something that has been, until recently, largely unknown to the populace, especially in regard to girls. This state of coping with something known to us, but foreign to others comes with added stressors.

Stressors = strain = crankiness = reflexive coping mechanisms kicking in = ???

Coping mechanisms make all the difference in the world with regard to levels of perceived stress and anxiety—and our relationship. Andrew likes to ruminate, I like to talk things out. Thankfully, we both like to think situations through, getting to the root whenever we can, trying to take an objective viewpoint. We also do our best to work out any difficulties before going to bed at night.

We have countless pressures on us as a couple as a result of Kristina's diagnosis. In truth, many stressors can be extrapolated from other portions of this book. For instance, regular school meetings are a stress in and of themselves. Unexpected calls home from school add to the pressures. Trying to convince the school of the accuracy of your child's diagnosis is intense. Interacting with people who refuse to wrap their heads around Asperger's causes much stress and frustration. Knowing your child is becoming the teasing target at school is heart wrenching. Trying to discern Asperger's outbursts from typical kid behavior isn't always easy to do.

Then there is the financial stress. I have stayed home longer than expected due to the number of Asperger's-related appointments, etc. I have no regrets, but it is safe to say that that choice has lessened any savings. Dealing with the health care system is not joy, especially when co-pays eat at your bank account. Add to that weekly co-pays for allergy shots, a sickness or two, and tanks of gas driving here, there, and everywhere. Don't forget the cost of visiting family, who live out of town. It all adds up fast.

There can also be stress on time if we find ourselves running here and there for this service or that meeting. (Generally, we have not had much stress in that area.) As we all know, it is near impossible to schedule all doctor and therapist visits in the evening and on weekends.

This means that work schedules need to be flexible, or one parent takes time off to make the appointments.

Again, this is what we have experienced. Some people have a great network of friends and/or family nearby who have flexible schedules, and, as a result, are able pitch in here or there. Others have financial security, with co-pays a mere blip on the screen. Some home school, so do not have the public school bureaucracy to work through. Some handle it all on their own, with an uncooperative spouse. In general, as for the concept of specific stressors, one size does not fit all, but the concept of stress does extend to most.

Ah…stress and marriage. I can hear some quip, "Marriage *is* stress!" Still, others are waving and shouting at me, "Do you think having an Aspie in the family means endless stress and strain? How *dare* you!"

Whoops. That wasn't my intention.

There are many benefits to having a daughter with Asperger's. Among such is living with someone with a unique perspective on the world. However, to ignore the reality of stress on a marriage with a super-special child does a disservice to those wanting to understand what others are going through. Sometimes, simply knowing that someone else has "been there" too, can provide the encouragement to face another day. Also, stress on a marriage does not mean that the marriage is in jeopardy. Not at all.

However, I would argue that how the partners handle stress may contribute to that factor.

All in all, I feel fortunate that I have a strong marriage.

Asperger's in Pink

When Andrew and I were dating, we found solace in the mundane: chores, shopping, and simply sitting side by side. We always fancied ourselves as teammates. When life gets tough, Andrew will remind me that we do work very well as a team. We need to look at life's curve balls from that perspective.

He's right.

When Kristina received the diagnosis of Asperger's Syndrome Disorder, we sat and talked for a while. We discussed what it all meant. We simply rambled and listened to each other. We didn't look at the other, affixing any sort of blame, as others might. We moved forward as a team, as a unit.

Our first task was to decide if, when, and what to tell family. We discussed strategy. We knew some family members would be critical, others accepting, and some confused. After speaking with the critical branches of the family, we simply vented. Neither of us takes our attitudes as a personal reflection on the other. I hope this is a common attitude for couples to share. Unfortunately, I am sure it is not universal. Truthfully, visiting extended family can be a source of stress for the reasons mentioned earlier. However, generally speaking, those times tend to strengthen and bond us. The same goes for school.

I guess it's when our guard is down that we have the most difficulty. For instance, going out to eat can be unpleasant. If we can't eat at "that" place, sit in "this" booth and order certain kinds of food, then the legs fall off the proverbial table, and all bets are off. We have a saying in our home, "When any of us is hungry, we get cranky." So, if we are already hungry, and something doesn't go as planned, we are apt to get cranky.

Consider this chain of events: Kristina has to sit at a table, instead of a booth. She is already hungry, so she gets grumpy. Andrew is hungry, too. He hears her complain, and watches her expressive body language, and becomes embarrassed and frustrated. As he is hungry, it is harder than normal to be patient. As I see the events unfolding in front of me (and I'm hungry, too), I strive for peace like crazy. I do what I can to control the situation, which may be too overbearing, leading to further crankiness. Neither Andrew nor I are happy with the evolving situation. At home, we may be frustrated with how the other handled it all. We may also feel like eating out peaceably is just one of those things we'll have to shelve, except for date nights. To us, eating out should be a normal, laid back, family experience. Since our expectations are not met, it feels like something has been taken from us. So, the next time one of us suggests eating out, the other may cringe, causing tension between us both. This inevitably leads to a discussion.

Got to love those marital discussions.

Another aspect that is difficult for us is our mutual desire to hermit. Andrew works long hours, like most folks. When he comes home, he wants solace. As I now work from home, when he comes home, I need to talk. At the end of the day, however, Kristina sets the tone. All in all, time and experience have taught us to understand when it is Asperger's getting in the way, or merely being human.

Life and time have taught us to decrease, if not do away with our expectations. We also have learned to compromise, and even let go of certain things once considered family time.

One such sacrifice is eliminating the habit of going out to eat regularly, especially at new places, or those with different cuisines. Aside from the cost, it just isn't worth it. Some people have chided us for choosing to do so, saying we are letting Kristina run our lives. To the contrary, going out, even to a place she enjoys, can be rife with anxiety. At this point in our lives, it just isn't worth the added stress to try a new place as a family. There are some areas we push. This is not one of them.

We know the triggers for each family member, and respect them.

Sporting events are another activity that we shelved early on. The lights, periods of darkness, loud music and horns are simply too much for a kid like Kristina to handle. Even with earplugs, the sensory soup can be overwhelming. As Andrew is a sports fan, it's been tough, especially when you have season tickets one year, and go without the next. I'm not a huge fan, so missing out on hockey or baseball isn't such a big deal to me. However, it is something we used to do frequently, and Andrew feels the loss. We don't go on many dates (for various reasons, cost being one of them), and the suggestion of hockey over a dinner out isn't very appealing to me—especially when my idea of a dinner out involves fine china, candlelight, and soft music. Again, feeling the loss of that sort of time together, and the lack of a poker face, it's easy to see his disappointment. Craving a peaceful meal out, I don't do well compromising. He senses that, and is understandably disappointed. As neither of us is happy with what the other wants to do, the night out is bagged. The result is another mundane night at home, with Kristina sometimes giving us anything but private conversation.

That's not good.

In fact, giving up on working it out, we lose much needed time alone. We spend so much of our time using social stories, explaining situations to Kristina, and other things (like work, etc.), there often seems little energy left for us. So, when a potential conflict arises, it's hard to muster the energy to face it and work through it. That does not mean we avoid these situations. It just means we are worn out, and don't feel up to making another lap. As Kristina gets older, we find we need to do less explaining and teaching. As a result, our mental energy is increasing.

When we do go out on dates, we try to choose something that will allow us time to talk uninterrupted. Our most successful dates generally consist of quick bite, and running a few errands.

Errands?

Yes, errands. Shopping with Kristina is a very different experience than shopping with just the two of us. It has even been enjoyable at times.

No, really.

In all honesty, we live a simple life. In doing so, our creativity has taken flight. Let's face it, no matter what your budget may be, sometimes, you just cannot get a sitter, but you really need date time. For those times, we plan a date night at home. We tell our daughter it's a date night, and she honors it. We'll feed her an early dinner, and set her up with a movie, while we have some together time. Kristina has always been respectful of in-home date nights. In fact, sometimes she will play the role of hostess, as we begin our evening together.

Although Andrew's schedule varies greatly, we also manage a few lunch dates during the school year. The bottom line is we learned to take the time when and where we could get it.

As for our relationship, I truly think our constant view of each other as teammates makes all the difference in the world. Building on the concept of being a team, we share responsibilities around the house. Although I do the bulk of the housework, Andrew pitches in whenever he senses I need a break. He's not above doing dishes, nor I the taking out the trash. We work very well together.

We also understand each other's love language, how we demonstrate love, and how we best respond to it. That, alone, helps us understand each other on a deeper level.

Having the same faith foundation has truly helped us through many a rough spot. In all honesty, there are days you have to look at life through the eyes of faith for it to make any sense at all.

Looking back over Kristina's youngest years, I wish I would have squeezed out a few more dates here or there. If I were granted one wish in relation to our marriage, I would have wished for one long weekend away each year. Maybe there were people who would have watched Kristina for us, and I simply never identified them. However, when your child struggles with certain areas of life, you can't help but wonder if it would have worked out okay. You don't want to be a bother.

If I could speak to those supporting families of super special kids like Kristina, I would say this: speak up if and when you are willing to take the kid(s) for a weekend. Let the parents know you are serious, and that the kids will not be a burden. Some folks need that extra boost of confidence to take that step. We sure did.

All in all, we do all right. We're still a team, and plan to keep it that way.

And I still catch myself smiling each time he pulls into the driveway, home from a long day at work.

PINK PEARLS

for Chapter One

FOR THE COUPLE

· ·

Know the triggers

Know each family member's triggers, and respect them. Is it hunger? Exhaustion? Spontaneity?

Understand each other's coping mechanisms

Is one of you a talker, and the other a thinker? Respect the differences.

Don't play the blame game

Resist the urge to pin your child's Asperger's on anyone. If markers are seen in those around you, take it as an opportunity to understand them better, much as you desire others to understand your child.

The strain on time, energy, and finances is REAL

Acknowledge added stressors, but don't let them take over.

Additional stress does not presume the marriage will fail

Stress, good or bad, is a part of life. However, if the stress becomes too much to bear, or coping mechanisms become unhealthy, please seek professional help.

View each other as teammates

Be a helpmate to your spouse. Take a "team" approach, and try to be as objective as possible. Look at difficulties as strength builders—not sappers

Edit your expectations

Take time together whenever you find it. Are you able to meet for lunch? Even a few minutes alone, talking uninterrupted, can fuel the marriage.

Fix (firm up) the foundation

Make time to be together. Be willing to reinvent current concepts of "date nights."

Take advantage of offers from friends and family to watch the kid(s)

If offers to watch your child are sincere, and come from people you deem reliable and trustworthy, take a deep breath and say, "Yes. We'll do it." Then leave the guilt on the doorstep. Trust them to contact you if there are any problems, and enjoy your together time.

FOR FRIENDS AND FAMILY

. . . .

Speak up with sincerity

Make sure the caregivers understand your sincerity when you offer to take the kids for a bit. They may worry about imposing on you, and need reassurances that everything will be okay. Set up a way to communicate with them for peace of mind.

Look for ways to help

Could you pop by, and watch the kids while the caregivers go for a walk? Could you play a game with the child while mom cooks dinner?

Accept the quirks

Understand that quirks are part of the package. Avoid the temptation to "fix" whatever you consider problematic in the caregivers' parenting style—or even relationship. Be a loving, patient friend.

I WISH...

. . . .

I had arranged more date nights out, as well as an overnight each year, despite the cost (or worries) at the time.

INSIDE the
BUBBLE

That Empathy Thing, Again

"I can't wait for 7:30!" exclaimed Kristina. "Tonight is a new episode!"

Andrew shot me a look.

"Don't worry," I said, "We have time if we leave soon."

"Where are we going?" asked Kristina.

"We're going to the hardware store tonight to look at a few things."

"Why would you ever want to go to that place?" complained Kristina.

"The store is going out of business, and we're going to check a few things that are on sale," I respond.

"Don't worry," reassured Andrew, "we'll be home in time for your show."

"Why do I have to go? Can't you stay home with me, and Mommy can go by herself?"

"We're going as a family," I affirmed.

This should be fun. Anytime we go to a store Kristina has no interest in, she does her best to verbalize her protests during the entire excursion. This should be no exception.

A short ride later, we pulled into the parking lot.

"Why is there a sale sign here?" asked Kristina.

"The store is closing," says Andrew.

"Woo-hoo!" Kristina cheered.

"Kristina," I try, "many people are losing their jobs."

"So?"

"Kristina, that's not a good thing."

"So what if this store closes?"

"All of these stores are closing," Andrew said.

"All of them? For how long?" asked Kristina.

"For good."

Kristina's shallow joy turned quiet. For a moment, it seemed to sink in that this was bigger than simply one store closing, leaving one less uninteresting place for her to have to go on errands.

As we entered the store, a twinge of sadness hit. These stores have existed as long as I have lived in North Shore. Sure, some argue that they ate up the little guys along the way, and now it's their turn to be the consumed by even bigger fish. Still, these are more local jobs lost. One more store to shut down. However, our money is tight, and we needed to take advantage of these sales. Still, I couldn't help but feel melancholy as I entered this place.

"I want to see the kid stuff," declared Kristina.

"Not yet, we need to look for a few things first."

"I want to see the kid stuff."

"We are going to look at tiles first."

"We are not getting a new kitchen floor because the old one is perfectly fine and is slippery, which is what I need to practice my skating in the kitchen."

The kitchen floor is not fine. Years have gone by, the tiles have yellowed, cracked, and become scratched. We want to sell soon, and we need to replace the flooring. This is change, and Kristina wants none of it. So, it has become her duty to do what she can to stop the change.

"Well, Kristina, why don't you help us look at tiles?" we calmly asked.

"We're not getting new tiles. You will ruin the kitchen."

A few shoppers glanced our way as they heard Kristina protesting our presence in the flooring aisle. Some looked disapprovingly at us.

Ignore them. Let it go.

Andrew led me to a few samples to consider. There weren't many designs left, but the prices were too good to pass up, since replacing the flooring at regular prices was out of the question. Kristina quieted a little, and maypoled around me. I didn't even worry about what others might have thought as they saw a nine-year-old circling around her mother. Kristina is quiet and calm when she rotates around me.

We gave up on the tiles and moved on to other sections of the store. Along the way, Kristina became attached to several sale items, including a very long plastic bench. Tears filled her eyes as we told her we weren't buying it. She remained glued to the seat, tears streaming down her face, as shoppers passed along. We remained calm and matter-of-fact as we stood firm against buying the bench. Finally, Kristina spied another desirable item, and the bench was forgotten.

I have a dream that one day we will spontaneously go to a store without one complaint from Kristina. Until then, we have to muddle through. Some may try to encourage us, saying she will be grown one day, and we will once again be able to shop where we want, at what speed we want, without her around to complain. Some say get a sitter and be done with it. I call the latter self-centered and lazy. Both miss the point. I want to do things, in harmony, with my family, and Kristina is part of my family. Andrew and I are going to keep trying, even if that day never comes.

Soon enough, we are home. It is 7:30, and Kristina is glued to the TV. I can feel more gray appear on my head. But I'm okay.

Finally, it's bedtime. The routine begins again. I unbutton my flannel outer-shirt so I can get a goodnight hug from my princess. Her hugs are like none other. Her tight, warm grasp and smile melt the frustrations of the day away. I love my daughter with all of my heart. I believe she loves me, too. I am thankful that Andrew and I can see her huge, warm heart. We know it's there. We believe in her.

Chapter Ten

Winning the Daily Battles

DADDY: *"How are you feeling today?"*

KRISTINA: *"I'm okay, I guess,"*

DADDY: *"Just okay?"*

KRISTINA: *"We'll, I'm not sick, so I guess I'm feeling okay."*

Some folks want a mansion to fill their need for status. Others want one to feel spoiled, much like a king or a queen. I want a grand mansion, with sprawling hallways so my husband and I can have a private conversation.

Although Kristina goes to bed on time, she does not require much sleep. Living in a small house makes it nearly impossible for Andrew and me to have a private conversation while Kristina is awake. Too many times to count, Andrew and I have mistakenly assumed Kristina is sleeping, only to hear her shout something from her room regarding whatever we are discussing.

Once Kristina turned ten, Andrew bought her a boom box for Christmas. Initially, we were concerned she was making herself stay awake, listening to her favorite music. Then the light came on. Ever since she began going to bed to the radio, she stopped interrupting our evening chat.

Life with Kristina is never dull. In many ways, living with Kristina is akin to living with a lie detector. Or a truth transmitter. Or a loudspeaker.

I learned the hard way never to complain about a haircut if my daughter is coming along for the next one.

"Mommy, is this the woman who gave you a bad haircut?" asked Kristina, sitting in the small rattan chair, four feet away from my hairdresser.

"Kristina, I never said that. I said it was just a little short last time, that's all."

"No, you said that it was the worst haircut you ever had."

Kristina no longer goes with me to get my haircut.

I also learned to give a good, clear reason for the times I don't want to—or can't—be on the phone.

"Hi, Grandma, no, Mommy's here, she just doesn't want to talk to you right now…I don't know. She told me she doesn't want to talk to you, or Grandpa right now…No, she's not sick. She's sitting on the couch… Mommy, why are you staring at me?"

I also learned the hard way to use hand signals or written notes, instead of touch, to get Kristina's attention. One Sunday morning, Kristina was a bit squirmy and noisy during a solemn church service. I gently tapped her on the leg in an effort to get her attention.

Kristina translated the tap as a hit (something I should have assumed would be the case), then transmitted it—to the entire congregation.

Kristina, at full volume, exclaimed, "Mommy, why did you *hit* me?"

"I did not hit you," I whispered back.

"Yes, you did!" Kristina continued, with no change in her tone, "You *hit* me on the leg! You did it on *purpose*!"

I should have left her to her noisy restlessness. It would have been less distracting.

Live and learn.

Of all of life's obligations, when it comes to Kristina, self-control, and over-stimulation, grocery shopping takes the cake.

As a stay-at-home mom, I am able to do the bulk of our grocery shopping during the school day. As a stay-at-home mom, when school isn't in session, I do the bulk of our grocery shopping with Kristina. Needless to say, grocery stores aren't what they used to be, especially the one by us.

Our grocery store is a Cadillac among grocery stores. Sure, you can buy milk and eggs, but there is so much more. At our grocery store, you can sit down in the café, and have lunch. On the way to buy toothpaste and soap, you can drop off your dry-cleaning. You can even rent a carpet steamer, if you are so inclined.

But that's not all.

Our grocery store has a magazine selection that rivals any bookstore. In fact, it contains its own sort of bookstore, including all sorts of products geared toward kids, including small plushies.

Kristina loves going grocery shopping.

To Kristina, grocery shopping means lots and lots of things to buy—none of which will ever make it to the dinner table. It means honing ways to have her mother break down and purchase all sorts of new, gleaming things for her.

For me, grocery shopping with Kristina is an exercise in saying "no."

Every other aisle seems to contain some product Kristina simply cannot live without. At first, I used to explain to Kristina why I would not buy all these things for her every time she asked for them. Sometimes, I just said "no." Thankfully, we came to a compromise. We agreed she could use her allowance to make purchases, limiting most of her pleadings. Like most other things in life, arriving at that modus operandi came after learning the hard way.

When Kristina was around eight, she went about her usual routine, asking for anything that caught her eye. As the "no's" increased, so did her level of emotion. By the end of the trip, Kristina was in tears. As we approached the checkout lane, I implored her to relax, and let it go. As the cashier rang up our order, she looked at Kristina, then at me, and asked, "Is everything okay?" Before I could answer, Kristina, cried out, tears flowing, "No! Everything is *not* okay!"

I was mortified.

The cashier looked confused, seemingly not knowing what to think.

I muttered something, though I can't remember what.

At home, Kristina and I discussed the situation, with no immediate solution. Honestly, afterwards I went to my room, and cried. Some days, regardless the knowledge of the equation: overstimulation + Kristina + difficulty with self-control = meltdown, my skin simply is not thick enough to handle it all.

On the whole, our life is fairly routine. Kristina is, in many ways, a typical kid. Contrary to what others may think, we do not perpetually make excuses for her behavior. Not all of her negative behaviors are due to sensory integration, difficulty with self-control, or her way of looking at the world. Sometimes, Kristina makes poor choices. Sometimes, Kristina gets in trouble.

Sometimes, it's not a matter of being able to "think it, not say it," but a matter of choosing to yell, or something else, in an effort to get her way. Like any other kid, she is fully capable of making wrong choices, resulting in a negative consequence. Finding the right consequence to fit the sin has been an effort in trial and failure.

Andrew and I took a parenting class when Kristina was quite young. Most of what we learned was ineffective. So many of the suggestions never worked with our daughter. As time went by, and we learned about Asperger's, we discovered our parenting style would most likely differ from neurotypical parenting. The old "because I said so" never registers with Kristina. Neither does a quiet stare.

Think about it, a quiet look evokes the need to decipher it accurately, something Kristina is still working on.

We have tried various disciplinary methods, including time out. The most effective method to date is one tied to the behavior itself. If Kristina says something unacceptable, or uses an unacceptable tone, we choose a consequence that fits. Since she chose to use her mouth (speaking) for the offense, she will most likely lose dessert that evening. If she uses her hands in a negative manner, the consequence will entail using her hands for a specific chore, etc. Simply put, we tie the negative behavior to the offending body part.

Kristina has latched on to this method of discipline. In fact, she tries to make it apply to us, as well—when *she* sees fit. For example, we work with Kristina about not pointing.

The thing is, we left out the part about "at people."

Kristina being Kristina, translated the words "don't point" literally. One day, I pointed to something in the house, and Kristina became quite upset with me, fussing at my abhorrent behavior, as I had said not to point.

Kristina is very adept at pointing out our flaws.

Sometimes, my frustration is a result of my choice of wording, and Kristina's subsequent interpretation. One morning, before school, Kristina asked to swing a little before we left. No problem! However, when I told her it was time to go, she said "okay," but continued to swing. Once again, I told her it was time. Again, she said, "okay," but kept on swinging. I called to her several times before she stopped, understandably frustrated. As she approached the car, I asked her why she chose not to come when I called to her. She responded that she knew it was time to go, but was having more fun swinging. The reason she said "okay" was to let me know she heard me, not that she was going to stop swinging.

We straightened that out.

In general, although much of life hums along like that of any other family, we have made adaptations and alterations as to how we view our life as a family unit. Just as we no longer participate in certain outings with friends, we avoid other outings, as a family.

Of all the things crossed of the "typical family fun time" list, movies are at the top, second only to fireworks. The dark room, huge screen, and loud volume are very overwhelming for Kristina. It took well into fourth grade for Kristina to sit through her first movie, and enjoy it. It is still difficult to convince her to go to the theater, even though her past few experiences have been positive. Going to the movies is something we don't take for granted.

In general, we focus on creating family time around the house, as opposed to hopping in the car and heading somewhere. Most nights, we try and carve out some family time, even if only for a few minutes. Family time is something we all look forward to, and miss when our schedules are hectic. Family time has an added side benefit; it is helping instill in Kristina the fact that her parents love her, enjoy her, and want to spend time with her. This facet has become especially important, as the gap between her and her peers increases. Playing together also works as time to focus on sportsmanship, as she is quite competitive, still working on the skill of being a good loser—and winner.

Like all kids with Asperger's, Kristina's special interests invade all parts of life, including family time. It is something we have come to expect. Kristina is incredibly creative. She loves adapting board games to fit her current special interests, adding twists here or there to better suit the theme (usually physically recreating entire board games, in order to make them "work." This includes making a brand new board, new cards, new tokens, etc.). Sometimes, we watch her current DVD favorite, or play "character guess-it," revolving around her favorite movie or TV show at the time. We really don't mind.

It's funny when we try to explain special interests to others. On the surface, saying that a child has a special interest in a particular thing, like a TV show, isn't surprising. Mentioning that she has seen every episode, and collects the figurines hardly raises an eyebrow. But when you mention your child has *memorized* every episode, to the letter, people start to take notice. (Kristina prides herself on memorizing movies the first time she sees them.) Add to that the creation of complete magazines and fun books revolving around the special interest, and a few other odds and ends, and the difference between a typical interest and a special interest becomes clearer.

I have to admit, some special interests are better than others. When she was in her Lilo and Stitch phase, we had it good. With hundreds of experiments to memorize, several movies, and loads of TV episodes, this one took a while to tire of. About three days after it was replaced with a different animated movie (with no TV episodes, and no other depth), we were begging for its return!

In general, my daughter's interests tend to revolve around animals and Disney movies—generally those with animal stars. Over time, her specific special interests have changed. This is especially the case with TV shows and movies. But through it all, her love for animals remains strong.

Kristina is a true lover of animals; stuffed, printed, painted, and otherwise. Her love is not restricted to the fluffy and cuddly, either. Our daughter has developed a fascination for the scaly, including snakes, and even dinosaurs. Her interest in animals brings a whole new meaning to the term "well-rounded."

Kristina being Kristina, our daughter never took to dolls. She has a few she loves, but they largely remain on the shelf. They are special to her, but nothing near her love for her stuffed animals. (Her American Girl® dolls are an exception, though they still rank far below her "S.A.'s," as Kristina refers to them.)

Kristina's attention to detail is staggering. Her ability to memorize movies on the spot is unmatched. Not to mention that she has her own unique sense of style. She is a very complex girl.

Despite all this, I can't get her to follow more than one direction at a time.

Go figure.

As I mentioned earlier, Kristina's form of play mimics life. Her favorites include birthday celebrations (for her stuffed animals) and school (for her stuffed animals). For as long as I can recall, Kristina has played "birthday." As Kristina grows, so does the level of detail in her play. She has good manual dexterity, and has a knack for crafting. She uses that skill to create party hats, paper plates, and goodie bags—filled with paper favors and candy. One evening, while she was in the middle of making favors for the latest goodie bags, we needed

Kristina to switch gears. She complained, even cried a little, as I told her she needed to stop so we could move on with the plans for the evening. We agreed on a stopping point, cutting out miniature paper strips of gum, which helped lessen her anxiety. As she was cleaning up, a thought dawned on me. As far as I could remember, Kristina never seemed to play in the air.

Here's what I mean. Like most women, I spent many of my teen years babysitting. Much of that time was spent pretending with those children. We pretended to sip tea out of pretend china cups. We pretended to throw imaginary balls all over the living room. We pretended to catch them, even slip on them. It was a hoot.

As far as I could recall, save one imaginary game played outdoors in the summer, Kristina never played in the air. As far as I could remember, Kristina protested each time I suggested to her we play like that. It was unthinkable for her to play with imaginary food for those parties, or imaginary desks and pencils for school. Substituting chenille stems for pencils was likewise unacceptable.

A little while back, while I was in Kristina's room, I noticed the school passes Kristina created. On the front, she drew a picture of the S.A., along with the last name, and the name of the pretend school. On the back of the tag, she wrote the date of hire, along with the address of the school. I have to wonder if that is the same information on the tags the personnel at her school wear around their necks.

In light of this reflection, I decided to ask her what she thought of imaginary play. As I discussed this concept, her face soured, she raised her eyebrows, and told me that idea was totally objectionable, and made no sense. It also made her feel uncomfortable.

It clicked. In order for Kristina to enjoy play, she truly has to mimic life. This does not mean simply throwing a party with guests, and *imagine* this, that, and the other thing. It means *physically* replicating those things for play. Her concept of *imagining* included *pretending* the paper goodie bags, and paper candy (which she can touch and see) as the real thing.

As she grows older, she has been able to modify her school play to either exclude parts she does not care for, or to include her own preferences. Although she no longer strictly adheres to replicating her current real-life classroom experience, she still creates an authentic setting. Kristina is one for detail. Such play provides an interesting view into her world.

So much of Kristina being Kristina is replete with paradox. It never ceases to amaze me how she can memorize all sorts of things at first glance, replicate others with exacting detail, yet forget library day. Her room is a visual chaos, despite regular neatening, and her love of sorting. (Kristina refers to it as organized chaos.) She is quite particular about how she dresses for school, yet refuses to look in a mirror. She has a very limited, bland palate, but adores broccoli. She struggles with the concept of empathy, yet has one of the biggest hearts I've ever run across.

Raising Kristina has been the most complex emotional ride of my life. The highs and lows all come with unexpected twists and turns. Raising Kristina, I have learned so much more about human nature, about myself, even, than I ever envisioned possible. Her way of looking at life has me questioning some of our societal norms. My daughter is a beautiful blossom, wanting to bloom in the dead of winter. With teamwork, love, endurance, and faith, we look forward to watching her flourish. We believe she will.

Kristina is making it amidst the neurotypicals. We know she can succeed throughout life, though it won't be without struggle. She is a fierce competitor. We will continue to support her, to help her reach the point where she can tackle life on her own. We are confident she will one day, when alone and faced with life's storms, be able to right herself and swim to shore.

After all, that is what matters.

PINK PEARLS

for Chapter Ten

FOR THE CAREGIVERS

Those very special special interests

Special interests are as much as a part of Asperger's as living and breathing. Your active interest in her interests will put a sparkle in her eyes!

You can't write everything off

Sometimes, bad behavior is simply a kid being…well…a kid. The tricky part lies in determining what is Asperger's, and what isn't.

Becoming behavior

Each child is different, Asperger's or not. In light of that, find what behavior modification works for the individual child—and be consistent with it. Don't be afraid to contact a qualified therapist, who can work with you and your child, and provide you with suggestions and tools.

Mind the meltdown

Meltdowns due to over stimulation are the rule, rather than the exception. Make sure you have a plan in place to address such situations before leaving for the store. A good plan may greatly lessen the chances for a meltdown to occur—or at least the intensity of one.

Let her sort it out!

Coupons, that is. If your daughter likes to sort, let her sort and file the grocery coupons.

Embrace the routines

As much as "pasta night" gets old quickly, it also lends stability in a crazy world. Establish healthy routines, which help your child have an anchor in the day-to-day. Routines may become, well, routine, but they are a much better family alternative than living the sporadic life.

Find family time

Carve out some time on a regular basis for family time. Even when time is tight, playing just five minutes of a "guess it" game can be good for everyone.

FOR OTHERS

Yes, she really does know the individual colorway and eye angle of all her 200+ mini bobble-headed toys—and their individual collector numbers.

Think it, don't say it.

Or roll your eyes. When in public, watching a meltdown, resist the urge to "fix" the situation—or the parent. Most parents are well aware of the situation, and are uncomfortable enough, as it is. A knowing smile, or kind word, works wonders, more so than a "constructive comment," no matter the intent.

Have a special interest

Do you know the child's special interest(s)? Engage the child by asking about it. It may just be the key to opening their social interaction combination lock—even briefly.

I AM THANKFUL FOR

My beautiful, humorous, passionate, creative daughter, and her unique way of navigating this path that we call life.

Thursdays with Tori

"Mommy, that shirt makes you look pregnant."

One way I differ from the average woman is my dread of haircuts. I don't know why; I always feel better after a trim. Maybe it's the last-minute feeling of needing to be somewhere, and getting the date all wrong. Maybe it's a subconscious fear of repeating that bad cut in second grade.

The one where my mom decided my waist-length hair was better traded for a pixie cut.

The one where I looked like a boy for over a year.

Not that there is anything wrong with that.

Unless you are a girl who wants to look like a princess, as I did.

My anxiety truly is unfounded. You see, haircuts make the best therapy. I don't need to provide an insurance number. The total cost is the same as a co-pay. I don't even have to wait three months for my first appointment. And, if I exceed a certain number of haircuts, I won't be penalized.

Just like Kristina's therapy, the benefit of the haircut lies in the skill of the worker.

And I'm not talking about cutting hair, either. I'm talking about listening.

Enter Tori. Sure, she can give a mean haircut. But that's not the main reason I go. Tori is one of those amazing women who have been there, too. Not only has she only "been there, done that," but, even though her family is grown, is still "doing it." When I talk about Kristina, she gets it. When she talks about her own family, I get it. When I tell her how upset I am with the school, she'll recount her own experiences, letting me know she believes me, and has been there, too. Her candor and openness teach me that life ahead may be smoother, but won't be without its own bumps and unexpected turns. She teaches me what I need to do now, as well as the things that most likely will not change with time. Tori is a treasure trove, full of compassion and understanding.

One day, I was lamenting the fact I had no one in town to confide in. Then I went for a haircut, and was reminded how lucky I truly was. Just as I prayed a prayer for Kristina, for one, solid friend, I prayed for myself. But it took me a long time to realize that God had answered that prayer. One Thursday morning, my eyes opened. Here she was, holding a pair of shears in front of a long mirror. God had provided someone all along.

It's funny how often we ask for things, only to find out they are just a little to the left of us. Sometimes our focus is so narrow we lose our peripheral vision. We lose our perspective on life. I hope that, somehow, even if only for a moment, my family has afforded you a broader perspective on Asperger's and girls. I hope that, someday, the next girl to waltz through the diagnostic door will be understood just as well as her male counterparts.

Or even more so.

Here's to raising my Kristina, and all the other girls made even more special by Asperger's Syndrome Disorder.

Here's to Asperger's, in pink.

PINK PEARLS

for Chapter Eleven

FOR MY HUSBAND

. . . .

Thank you for your patience, integrity, and sticking by me.

FOR AN UNNAMED FRIEND

. . . .

Thank you for the time, however brief, you listened and shared with me, and for taking me as I am, not who you wish I would be. I hope our paths will cross again.

FOR THE MASSES

. . . .

Know that our stories, our pain, our joys are real. Though you may never identify with the path we've been given, which we currently tread, thank you for trying to understand us, our journey.

I AM THANKFUL FOR...

· ·

...YOU, yes you, who are holding this very book in your hands, and who have taken time out of your day, your evening, to listen to the female voice of Asperger's, from one family's perspective.

Thank you.

INSIDE the BUBBLE

Hope for the Future

Such a humid night. The moist air wraps around me, simply clinging. I walk down my long driveway, and cross the street, searching for the best of mediocre viewing points. I peer through the tops of evergreens and maple trees, trying to catch a glimpse of pink flashes of light.

Golden bursts of light shoot upwards, barely higher than the trees. The pops and bangs aren't nearly as loud as I remember them. Bursts of blue, pink, and white continue to poke above the treetops. I stand in admiration, and simply watch. Andrew steps outside, but only for a moment. Kristina is inside, and, as far as we can tell, asleep. A car speeds through our neighborhood, temporarily disrupting the moment. Andrew heads back inside, and I stay to watch.

Wow.

Swirling, glimmering gold light encircled with blue. I have forgotten how beautiful fireworks can be. Only a few shoot high enough for me to see them fully. But that's okay—how many people can take a few steps from their home and see any at all?

The booms come quicker and louder. These are the sounds I remember. I cover my ears for a moment, and soon the flashes of light and bangs are gone. I head back inside with the bittersweet feeling that has been with me the entire time. It's hard to fully enjoy fireworks when your daughter fears them.

I start to speak to Andrew, then notice a blonde head with elbows protruding from it. It's Kristina. She's been awake the entire time. After a few hand signals and a few words, she believes us that the fireworks are over, and lowers her hands. Her fingers are stiff and sore from the past several minutes, but relief shines over her. Only sweat covers her brow. The dreaded weekend has ended, and she can relax for the remainder of the summer. She's made it through. Such a huge victory for Kristina.

"I'm really proud of you, honey!" I say. Andrew just stares, beleaguered. Small victories are often unkind reminders of the constant struggles we face as a family. We muster up the words and actions to encourage our daughter. Meanwhile, one more year has past where fireworks aren't a family experience. Still, Kristina appears braver, more resolute. Even so, a wave of melancholy sweeps over us. But, now, it's bedtime for Kristina.

As I go in to say "good night," her arms reach out for me. I beam, as she calls to me for a hug.

"Mommy, come here!" smiles Kristina, as she draws me in. "Pbbbt!" and she laughs and gives me a raspberry. "Try it on me, Mommy!"

"Oh, uh, I'll try....P...b..."

"No Mommy," she laughs, "that's not it. Try again!"

I can't get it. Oh, well. We both share a laugh and even-more rare hugs, then it's time for lights out and a good night's sleep.

Gosh, I love that kid. I remember being told how love will just overflow out of your heart for your child. I remember thinking these folks were crazy. Of course, I'll love my kid! But you mean to tell me I'll love her even more than anything, ever?

And "they" were right.

I'll do anything for my daughter. I will continue to advocate for her. I will continue to be her friend. I will choose to let her be responsible for her own actions and choices. I so hope, with all of my being, that she will grow up to be happy, healthy, successful, and loved by others.

Kristina is simply amazing. I am proud to call her my daughter.

Maybe next year we will try to see the fireworks as a family. Maybe not. In the grand scheme of life, missing a few fireworks shows doesn't count for much. Even so, in a few years, Andrew and I will be able to go see them together, if we wish. Life is so much more than fireworks and movies and buttons. Life is so much richer having a daughter like Kristina.

No regrets. So much love. So full and right.

Tiger's Big Game

A Short Story by Kristina

ABOUT THE CHARACTERS

TIGER: an orange cat, Chirpadee's sister
CHIRPADEE: a pink bird, Tiger's sister
MOM: a Persian cat
DAD: a bluebird
COACH: a white boy poodle
KIESHA: a gray girl cat with a white stripe on her face
POOF-POOF: Coach's daughter, a white poodle
SHELLBY: a girl turtle with pink markings on her shell
MATILDA: a gray girl cat
DIANA: a girl brown dachshund
REFEREE: Shellby's dad, a turtle with blue markings
PAULINA: a girl panda

Tiger's Big Game

It was the big day. Tiger's soccer team had advanced to the grand finals! They were playing the Comets. Tiger gulped down her berry cereal rapidly, and rushed to get her grass-stained jersey out of her sloppy closet. Chirpadee followed. She helped her rummage through the pile.

"Got it!" Tiger called.

Chirpadee flew up to her own room. She had to get her fan gear. She went up to her dresser and looked inside the middle drawer. There it was, right where she had put it. A t-shirt she had painted. It read "Go Stars, Go TIGER!!!!" She slipped it on and went to get her blue #1 foam pointer finger (The Stars' colors were light blue and white). She took out some plain white paper and a yellow crayon. Then she drew a small picture of a glimmering star. Next, she neatly cut the star out.

Chirpadee flew downstairs like a lightning bolt. She snuck into her parents' room, quiet as a mouse. She went to the craft box where her mom kept her safety pins. Chirpadee grabbed a medium-sized one and flew back up to her room. She took her Blue Jays cap off her hat stand. Then she pinned the yellow star over the Blue Jays' team logo.

Meanwhile, downstairs, Tiger slipped on her jersey. She looked at herself in the mirror. The number 1 was clearly written on the back. Above the 1 were the words "Pizza Ville." On the front was the Stars' team logo, a turquoise shooting star.

Tiger grabbed her purple soccer ball and ran to the front door. She grabbed the keys to the garage and went outside. After she got the soccer net out of the garage, she lined it up in the yard. Tiger practiced her free-kicks for a while. Then Chirpadee (all dressed up) came outside with the car keys. She opened the back door and placed her cap and foam pointer finger inside. Then she flew over to the yard and played 1-on-1 with Tiger.

In the end, Tiger won. Soon their parents came out of the house and put their gear into the trunk of the car. They ran over toward the yard and played a two-on-two game. Chirpadee and Mom won that one.

Dad checked his new watch at the end of the game. They had just enough time to make it! The whole family rushed to the car.

When they arrived at the 'Kidz Sports Center' Tiger ran towards her team in the soccer fields. The coach was talking strategy. The first line-up was: goalie- Tiger, offense- Kiesha and Poof-Poof, and defense- Shellby and Matilda. Diana sat on the sidelines.

The referee blew his whistle for the game to begin. It was a tiring beginning, but eventually the whistle blew for half-time. Tiger had blocked a good shot earlier, yet she let one slip through. Poof-Poof and Kiesha each scored a goal.

The coach only changed a bit of the line-up. Diana went in for Kiesha and Tiger switched places with Poof-Poof. The referee blew his shrieking whistle for the game to begin again, and the Stars rushed out on the field to join the red and black Comets.

The game went on, and it was tied. Only 15 seconds were left in the game! Diana stole the ball from Paulina, a Comet. She dribbled down the field. Diana passed the ball to Tiger with only 5 seconds left in the game! She hastily whammed the ball with her foot, aiming toward the net.

It went in!

The referee blew his whistle. "TIME!" he shouted. The Stars jumped up and down. Tiger screamed.

That night, lying in bed, Tiger remembered it all. The clock, the pass, the perfect shot. It was something she would never forget. Never.

The End

References and Resources

BOOKS

Attwood, Tony. *Asperger's Syndrome: A Guide for Parents and Professionals*. Jessica Kingsley Publishers, 1998.

Chapman, Gary. *The Five Love Languages*. Northfield Publishing, 1995.

Hoban, Lillian. *Arthur's Birthday Party*. HarperTrophy®, 1999.

Kirby, Barbara L. and Patricia Romanowski. *The Oasis Guide to Asperger Syndrome*. Crown, 2001.

(The OASIS website: www.udel.edu/bkirby/asperger)

Pipher, Mary. *Reviving Ophelia: Saving the Selves of Adolescent Girls*. Putnam, 1994.

Asperger's in Pink

ARTICLES

Attwood, Tony. "The Pattern of Abilities and Development of Girls with Asperger's Syndrome." In *Asperger's and Girls* (pp. 1-7). Future Horizons, 2006.

Bauer, Stephen. "Asperger Syndrome." 1996. Accessed on the Oasis @ MAAP website: http://aspergersyndrome.org/Articles.

Flora, Carlin. "The Girl with a Boy's Brain." *Psychology Today*, Nov/Dec 2006.

WEBSITES

DR. TONY ATTWOOD'S OFFICIAL WEBSITE
www.tonyattwood.com.au

RUDY SIMONE'S OFFICIAL WEBSITE
www.help4Asperger's.com

AUTISM ASPERGER'S DIGEST MAGAZINE
www.autismdigest.com

FUTURE HORIZONS, INC., WORLD LEADER IN BOOKS, DVDS, AND CONFERENCES ON AUTISM, ASPERGER'S, AND SENSORY PROCESSING DISORDER
www.FHautism.com

THE GLOBAL AND REGIONAL ASPERGER SYNDROME PARTNERSHIP (GRASP)
www.grasp.org

OASIS@MAAP

THE ONLINE ASPERGER SYNDROME INFORMATION AND SUPPORT (OASIS) CENTER HAS JOINED WITH MAAP SERVICES FOR AUTISM AND ASPERGER SYNDROME.

www.aspergersyndrome.org

"SENSORY FRIENDLY FILMS" IN CONJUNCTION WITH THE AUTISM SOCIETY OF AMERICA
www.autism-society.org/site/PageServer?
pagename=sensoryfilms

or

www.amcentertainment.com/SFF

SOUTHPAW ENTERPRISES® INC., A RESOURCE FOR SENSORY INTEGRATION DYSFUNCTION PRODUCTS
www.southpawenterprises.com

TEACCH PROGRAM
www.teacch.com

PSYCHOLOGY TODAY MAGAZINE
www.psychologytoday.com

WRIGHTSLAW, A RESOURCE FOR EDUCATION LAW, SPECIAL EDUCATION LAW, AND CHILD ADVOCACY
www.wrightslaw.com

OTHER

American Girl® is a registered trademark of Pleasant company

Beanie Babies® is a registered trademark of the TY company

John Deere

Gatorade®

Barbie® is a registered trademark of Mattel

Cadillac is a brand of General Motors

Lilo and Stitch are creations of Disney

Wilbarger Brushing Protocol, developed by Patricia
Wilbarger, M.Ed., OTR, FAOTA
(source:www.thetherapyplace.net/newsletter/3_2.htm)

The Body Sox™
More information is available on such websites as:
www.sensory-processing-disorder.com/body-sox.html

A Charlie Brown Christmas by Charles Schultz

I Love Lucy created by Desi Arnaz

"Radar Love," by Golden Earring, 1973

Index

Asperger's in Pink

About the Author

Julie Clark is a writer, artist, and mom of a daughter with Asperger's Syndrome, who possesses a strong desire to increase awareness and understanding of the "pink" in the autism spectrum. Julie holds a Bachelor of Arts degree in Communications, with minor studies in French and Studio Art. When she isn't writing or creating, she spends time doing volunteer work, running, and is a natural foods enthusiast. Above all, her favorite activity is spending time with her husband and daughter. Julie and her family reside in the South, enjoying ample sunshine and bright blue skies.

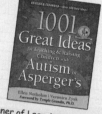